A TIME OF OUR LIVES

How we grew up from the 1940s to the 1960s

Gerald Rice

Published by
A Time of Our Lives Limited
11 Mornington Green, Trim, County Meath, Ireland.

Tel 00353 46 94 366 94   Mobile: 00353 86 03 150 84
(from outside Republic of Ireland)

Tel: 046 94 366 94   Mobile: 086 03 150 84

Email: info@atimeofourlives.com

Website : www.atimeofourlives.com

ISBN: 978-1-910179-12-3

Printed and Bound in Ireland by
eprint limited www.eprint.ie

A Time of Our Lives

is dedicated to a girl with nut-brown hair.

Thanks...

There are many people who have helped me to produce this book. Some of them are now dead. In the first instance I thank my parents, John and Lily (Elizabeth) Rice who showed love and good example to me throughout the years I also owe debts of gratitude to my relatives, teachers and many friends.

I want to thank Ben Brooksbank and Bill Nichols for permission to use their photographs of trains and a steamroller from the website www.geograph.org.uk, David Humphries for permission to use the bus and Morris Minor photos from the website www.outercirclebus.com and Kay Keane, a local artist in Trim, Ireland, who stepped into the breach and did the drawings of my grandad's Hillman Minx car and an ex-GPO van. Especial thanks are due to my son, Michael, for several photos and for his essential help with the complicated (to me) manipulations on the computer.

I would also like to thank my brother, Stephen and his wife, Anne, who have given much support over a long period; Paddy Smith who cast a professional and generally approving eye over my writing; to Bill Carson and Michael Munnelly for their comments on early drafts; to Ciarán Mangan, Meath County Librarian for his comments and support.

I would especially like to thank three people who unwittingly made this book possible and they are Di and Carl who each asked me a question which lead to the events of the second part of this book and Terry, without whom I probably would not have gone out on one particular night.

Above all, I want to thank the girl with nut-brown hair to whom this book is dedicated – she knows what for!

Contents

Introduction 1

Part One

Mario's War.. 7
1943 10
Early Years in Birmingham.. 11
Primary School Days... 19
A Letter To The Headmaster 25
Government Health Measures.................................... 29
Local Shops 31
Cigarettes and Cigarette Cards 34
Games... 35
More Shops 37
Christmas is Coming... 40
Memories of A Country Childhood 46
Summer Holidays... 48
My Holidays – Trains and Ships 49
Drumaness... 58
The Loop.. 65
Tales From The Loop 75
Back In Birmingham 82
Sport... 95
World Affairs 99
The Coronation 105
The Wireless...106
Comics, Books and The Pictures...............................112
Newspapers 118
1950s Predications 120

Smog...126

From Primary To Secondary School.................................127

In The Playground 133

Sports in School...136

Altar Servers..139

Leaving School, First Job - And A Blonde 144

Leaving School At Fifteen...147

National Service 148

College Years..150

Hitch Hiking In Ireland And Germany 162

Part Two

Going Out With A Second Blonde, Being Dumped and An Offer I Couldn't Refuse...168

En Route At Last and An Interesting Offer From Another Blonde
....173

A Good Turn For Yet Another Blonde, "Gun Running", Bobbee Moore - and Wanted By Interpol 181

With The Foreign Legion...187

You're Not Going To Believe This!...................................192

"We Were *British* Trained"...200

The Kano To Lagos Express..205

Homeward Bound..209

What Happened Next 212

Afterthoughts...220

Carl's Adventures in Canada..220

Questions And An Appreciation 222

A Request to Readers 225

How To Buy This Book..225

A TIME OF OUR LIVES

How we grew up from the 1940s to the 1960s

Introduction

I have often regretted that I did not ask my parents and grandparents what their lives were like when they were growing up and now much of what they knew and took for granted has been lost. My father and mother were both born almost 100 years before this book was written – my mother's father 136 years before. My father's father, born in 1891, worked in a linen mill as a *"rougher"* in 1911 and his thirteen-year-old sister worked in the same mill as a *"doffer"*. Neither of these jobs exist any more in this country and, while I might guess what a rougher did, I had no idea what a doffer's duties were until I searched on Google and discovered that she cleared heavy full bobbins from a spinning frame and replaced them with empty ones so that the machinery could continue spinning the linen yarn. How many similar changes have taken place since my grandparents were children that we no longer even know about?

This book is an attempt to preserve for my children and grandchildren, and anyone else who might be interested, something of what it was like to grow up between the 1940s and 1960s *(although there are some, perhaps many, who would say that I never grew up)*. I hope to show with examples from my own and others' experiences, how people, especially young people, lived in the period from the 1940's to the 1960's - or, the "olden times", that my children sometimes asked about when they were very young - and so bring to mind some of the happenings, sights, sounds and even smells of those days which were, in some ways, a golden time in which to be growing up in but an often difficult one for those already grown up.

The book is also intended, for those of a similar age to my own, to be a walk through the meandering lanes of memories of our younger days but also to give our children and grand-children an idea of a time when ten year olds could go off on their own, or with one or two friends, for hours at a time and no one would be worried about what had happened to them or concerned that they might have fallen into some danger. Few "Health and Safety" regulations existed but instead, common sense usually prevailed. This was a time when children played in the street without danger from the few cars around, when they listened to *Children's Hour* at five o'clock on the radio and, unless they were among the very, very few who had television at home, could only crowd round the windows of *radio* shops to watch the flickering black and white pictures of *Muffin the Mule* and of the Coronation in 1953 on small screen television sets.

It was a time when children enjoyed simple pleasures, not that much different from their parents and grandparents. If we wanted to meet friends, we went round to their houses to see if they were in. We couldn't call on a mobile phone, or even an ordinary land-line phone because very few people where we lived had such a thing in the house. We certainly weren't connected electronically 24/7 *(what a dispiriting expression)*. We couldn't text or tweet, so all contacts with our friends were face to face.

We found enjoyment in skipping stones across a pond, in not stepping on the cracks in the pavement, in building up pictures in our minds while listening to the *wireless* and, certainly in my case, in reading. Perhaps we benefited from using our own imaginations to amuse ourselves, rather than relying on a constant barrage of images from a screen. The world of my childhood was certainly slower and simpler than now but I think this meant that we had more time just to be children. It was a time when we were satisfied with having less because there was less to have.

This book is not intended as an autobiography, although, obviously, a considerable number of events of my life are included and the second part of the book tells of what was, for me, a very interesting and even exciting adventure in my early twenties. I hope you will also find it interesting. Rather than the book being an autobiography, I hope to show by episodes in my life and those of others what it was like to grow up in an aspirational and loving working class family, and many of these, and similar episodes, would have been part of the experience of growing up for many hundreds of thousands, indeed millions, of boys and girls around my age during the years about which I am writing.

The book is largely in chronological order but not rigidly so, as I remember aspects of growing up in connection with different topics covered, hence the *"meandering lanes of memories"* mentioned above.

PART ONE

Mario's War

Mario was born in 1931 and was eight when the Second World War started. He is twelve years older than I am and I first met him in 1962 when I started at College. His memories of growing up are very different from my own, his being coloured by the War years and, therefore, much more sombre than mine.

This is Mario's story (with some added comments towards the end of the section).

I remember in 1936 an airship (probably either the Graf Zeppelin or the Hindenburg) *passing low over our house in Leeds. I ran out to see it as it flew slowly over. My father, who was reading a newspaper in the house, refused to go out, saying that the time was coming when we would run in terror from such things. Two years later, in 1938, when I was seven, I remember talk about war with Germany being inevitable and I also remember that slit trenches were dug in many parks and other places as primitive shelters from the air raids expected at the start of war.*

As children left school in July 1939 for the summer holidays, we were told not to return in September but to listen to the news on the radio before doing anything. On September 1ˢᵗ, Germany invaded Poland and, starting on that same day, over 800,000 schoolchildren were evacuated from cities and towns all over Britain and moved to country areas where they would be safe from the air raids which were expected to start at any time. I was one of those children. Over 500,000 mothers and children under five and over 100,000 teachers were also evacuated.

My mother sat up all the Thursday night, sewing a haversack for me to take my clothes and preparing all the things I needed to take with me. This would be the first time I had been away from my family. My mother was too upset to take me to the school next day, so my great-aunt took me instead. Most of the pupils at my school were there and we climbed onto the buses with our haversacks or cases, an apple, an orange and our gas mask in a cardboard box. We had practised putting these on and we were told _never_ to be without these masks as gas attacks from the air were expected to be among the first actions of the war.

After what seemed like hours on the bus, we arrived in a small village and were taken to the village school – one room where all the children from four to fourteen were taught. We were lined up and adults came and chose which child or children they wanted to take. The Government paid five shillings (25p) a week for each child taken into a family. I was taken with another boy from my class by a family who had two boys about our own age (eight years old).

When school began, many lessons were taught in sheds, out-houses and hay lofts because the classroom was too small for the large numbers of new pupils. Our new "family" lived in the next village, three miles from the school, so we walked six miles a day. For me, it was like being transferred to the moon and I, like most others, hated it. Some children went back home after only a fortnight but I stayed for six long, dreary, hateful months. When I came back home to Leeds, my school was in turmoil because it had been turned into a First Aid Post. Half the teachers and pupils were still away in the countryside. We had air raid practices and gas mask practices but air raid shelters of any worth were slow in coming. Whenever the warning sirens sounded, we all moved into our cellar which was regarded as the safest place in the house. Back at my school, as at most others, retired schoolteachers returned to the classroom to replace the younger men and women who had been conscripted into the armed forces or auxiliary services. Some of those who returned were over seventy but they were still excellent teachers. Even so, the education of many, perhaps most, children was badly disrupted during the war years.

As the war continued, the effects of u-boat attacks on our shipping meant that everything which was rationed (that is, most things) became more and more scarce. The meat ration for a week for one person was the size of a chop. Butter, sugar, fats, eggs, meat and eventually bread and potatoes were rationed. Clothing was heavily rationed and, if you didn't have your ration "coupons" to hand over to the shopkeeper, you got nothing. As the war went into its fifth and sixth years, rationing got even stricter so that the weekly ration in 1945 for things like butter, margarine, cheese, bacon and clothes, among others, was only half (or even less) of what it had been in 1939.

(Even so, the diet of most people improved from before the War because the rationing of various foods took into consideration the provision of a healthy, if not an exciting, diet).

When the war ended, the people of Britain had very different ideas from those they had held in the thirties. Everyone, of whatever class, had suffered for the past six years. Even the "upper classes" had to put up with at least some aspects of rationing and some had their stately homes taken over by the army for training centres or to house evacuees. The royal family had their ration books, like everyone else.

Being wealthy or a member of the aristocracy did not prevent you from losing a father or mother, son or daughter, brother or sister in battle or in an air raid. There was a new idea of equality in spite of differences in social rank, a new impetus to sweeping away the poverty of so many which had marked the thirties in housing, education and health. It might take a long time to eradicate this poverty but there was general agreement that a start to achieve this should be made a national priority.

Not that everything improved suddenly or without difficulties. During the war, many women had worked outside the home for the first time, driving buses, working in factories or offices and earning their own money, many of them also for the first time. When their menfolk came back from war, looking to take over their old jobs again, there were difficulties and frictions, as many women returned to more traditional work, like teaching and nursing. There were also difficulties when young children saw their father for the first time in years and sometimes for the first time ever for those born when their father was away at war. But the social changes brought about during the war meant that things could not return to what they had been before.

Mario was fourteen when the Second World War ended but anyone born from 1942 onwards will have few, if any, direct personal memories of life during the Second World War.

1943

I was born on 7th July 1943 at a time when the largest tank battle in history was taking place. This was the battle of Kursk in Russia, over 1,700 miles from my birthplace in County Down in the northeastern corner of Ireland. I didn't take much notice of the battle at the time, being fully occupied with taking my first gasps of this strange new stuff called *"air"* but this battle was a decisive turning point in the course of the Second World War, marking the start of the German *Wehrmacht's* long retreat and the Red Army's advance through eastern and central Europe. The aftermath of the battle of Kursk was to form the background of my growing up during the Cold War period.

I was born in a farm worker's cottage in the middle of rolling countryside about 17 miles south of Belfast in County Down. Although I was born in July, I had made my presence felt before then. While my mother was pregnant, she took a craving for ice cream. This was a luxury not readily available in the countryside, in wartime, in 1943. So my father rode his bicycle 17 miles to Belfast, found a shop which sold ice cream, bought some and rode 17 miles back with it in a tin billycan. I suppose the can was packed round with straw or newspaper to stop the ice cream from melting. So, after a 34 mile round bicycle trip he presented the ice cream to his wife, only to be told she'd changed her mind and didn't want it any more. I never found out just what my father's reaction was! But I'm sure it was more restrained than many men's would have been because he was devoted to my mother and she was to him.

Unlike today, my christening was not a big family social event. I was baptised when I was just two days old. I went to the church in style, in a pony and trap, borrowed from one of the neighbouring farmers because there was no other transport available except a farm cart. There were very few cars and petrol was so strictly rationed that most of those cars stayed off the road for the six years of the War. I went with my godfather and godmother – my father's brother and my mother's sister. As was the custom then in that part of Ireland, neither my father nor mother was at the baptism, only my godparents.

Early Years in Birmingham

My father went to work in Birmingham as a motor mechanic shortly after the end of the war and my mother and I followed about nine months later, early in 1946. My parents rented a room in a large house owned by a very pleasant Indian couple and they were the only married tenants. The other people living there were all young single women, war refugees from various parts of Europe, who all took a liking to me. Well, I *was* only three years old - and cute at the time. Unfortunately, I have never been so successful with women again! Living in such a multilingual society, I was soon able to speak and recite nursery rhymes in French, German, Polish and Hungarian as well as English. However, my language skills quickly vanished when we left that house towards the end of 1946.

My father was a first class motor mechanic, like his own father but unlike either of his two sons. In 1945 he had returned to the garage where he had worked six years before and in the following year he was made foreman with five or six men working under him. His new position meant that we moved into a house attached to the garage in Villa Street, Lozells. This was a solid working class area about two miles north of Birmingham city centre and next to the then more middle class, or even posh, Handsworth. Nearer the city centre, the land rose and from there you could look over most of Lozells. You could see hundreds of houses closely packed together, half a dozen or more churches but very few trees. The nearest public green space was Handsworth Park, nearly a mile's walk away. Most of the houses in Lozells had been built between about 1840 and the end of the nineteenth century.

We lived in a street where most of the houses were like those in the opening credits of early *"Coronation Street"* episodes, except that these houses had a very small patch (maybe two or three feet) between the front door and the street pavement. Mostly, they were terraced "two up, two down" houses with the front door opening directly into the front room. Our house was one of a terrace of four larger houses set back from the street. These were built about 1840, with long narrow gardens at the front and a small walled back yard. Three steps led up to the front door, which opened into a hall about fifteen feet long.

The house was owned by the company which also owned the garage next door where my father was the foreman. The long, narrow front garden which the other three houses possessed had, in our case, been taken over completely by what would now be called the garage forecourt but what we called the garage "street". Here were parked the cars waiting for repair or collection and, just outside our front door was a hydraulic inspection ramp. The raising and lowering of the ramp provided endless fascination to me, as did the sight of the underside of the cars and vans inspected on it. I was also a bit scared of this ramp because when it was raised, there did not seem to be anything holding it up and I was always glad when my father or anyone else moved out from under it.

Our house was quite large but had only two rooms downstairs with a kitchen down three steps in the back extension and three bedrooms upstairs. It had no insulation or draught-proofing and the ceilings were high, so it was very hard to keep warm. The only heating was from a fireplace in each of the two downstairs rooms and a small basket fireplace in my bedroom.

One of the joys of childhood was when it was cold enough (that is well below freezing), or I was ill, to have the fire lit in my bedroom and I remember lying in bed in the dark looking at the flames and shadows flickering into magical shapes which always seemed so much better than the shapes you could see around you in the daylight world. Shapes like pirate ships, doors opening on to enchanted lands, even monsters. You could always get rid of these last by hiding under the bedclothes for a while but you would still check under the bed, just in case one was lurking there, maybe behind the chamber pot or *"guzunder"*, (so called because it "goes under" the bed), to grab the legs of an unwary six or seven year old. However, you had a good chance of escaping if you took a long stride or jump on to the floor when you got out of bed so that the monster(s) could not grip your ankles, since they did not move very quickly or far from the darkness under the bed.

When you did take that leap from the bed, you landed on the cold lino (linoleum) floor covering. Your first thought was to scramble back into the warmth of your bed, your second thought was that your mother had breakfast ready downstairs and your third thought was to find your socks and get them on before your now rapidly freezing feet fell off.

The downstairs front room was not used a lot, although we did have lodgers there from time to time. One of them, a friend of my father's, emigrated to New Zealand when I was about ten. I remember being impressed by the fact that he would be on the ship for six weeks and the journey would only cost him £10 (the cost of the voyage was subsidised by the New Zealand Government). I also remember a postcard from the Panama Canal – the first time we had ever received such a thing from that magical place, "Abroad".

The kitchen was three steps down from the living room, at ground level and, therefore, at a lower level than the rest of the house. It was a one-storey extension and contained a gas stove with an old gas mantle which was useful as a light source when the electricity failed. It had a rectangular, shallow, stone sink where my mother did the everyday washing. Eventually she got a gas heated wash boiler which had a mangle on top with two rollers and a handle which turned the two rollers linked by a pair of cog wheels. I can still recall the pungent but sweet smell of the *Oxydol* and *Persil* soap powders, which my mother used. When the clothes had been boiled, they would be rinsed in the sink and then put through the mangle to squeeze out the water. The only place for drying clothes was outside on the line in our back yard or inside on a wooden clothes horse in front of the fire in the living room.

Best clothes would be collected by the man from the *Court Steam Laundry* and delivered in a brown paper parcel tied with string three or four days later, freshly pressed and ready for my father and mother to wear to church on Sundays or for my father in his role as wicket-keeper for the parish cricket team. The grass stains on his immaculate white flannel trousers could only be effectively cleaned by the laundry.

A four-foot long tin bath hung on the wall in a short passage between the living room and the kitchen. Saturday was bath night with the bath in front of the living room fire and filled with hot water from the boiler in the kitchen. In later years, when I was in my teens, bath time became a visit to the municipal washing baths where a customer-*unfriendly* attendant would measure out a depth of maybe six inches of water before turning the tap off with a special key. Your time in the bathroom was also rationed. This was still a once a week ritual – if you had more than one bath a week, it was reckoned that you must be in love! Showers were exotic things that you only saw being used in Hollywood films and, even then, only in the most demure scenes.

Underneath the front room was the cellar where we kept the coal. This came in hundredweight (50 kg) bags made of very thick jute sacking and was a mixture of big and smaller lumps with some coal dust or *"slack"*. One of my jobs after the coal was dumped from the bags through the grating into our cellar was to break up the lumps into more manageable pieces with a hammer. This always took me a long time because the cellar was far enough away from my mother in the kitchen so that I could easily miss hearing her calling to me to hurry up and because the cellar was also our dumping ground for back copies of the daily papers with their cartoons, magazines and my comics, all of which proved so impossible to resist reading, that getting one bucketful of coal could easily take twenty minutes, or more.

The cellar also provided a home for several families of mice and hunting territory for our cat. Apart from the cat, the mice faced the additional hazards of mousetraps and of my mother's instructions to me to chase any mouse that appeared, hit it hard with the coal shovel and make sure it was dead by throwing it on the fire. Other pests, especially in summer, were flies and wasps. Fly sprays in handy aerosol containers were not common and the most usual weapons against these insects were rolled up newspapers and *flypapers*. These were long, sticky strips of strongly scented paper that could be pulled out of a small cardboard tube. They were hung from the ceiling and the flies and wasps would be attracted by the scent and were trapped by the sticky coating. When the whole strip was covered with dead insects, it would be thrown away and replaced. Flypapers were very effective but not very pleasing to look at.

My parents owned just three electric items, a radio (or *wireless*, as it was more commonly called), an electric iron and a small one-kilowatt electric fire. I don't think any other people in our street would have owned anything else electric. Indeed many country people, like my grandparents were still not connected to the mains electricity supply and if they did have a radio, it would be powered by a car battery, which needed charging from time to time at a garage. In many such homes in the countryside, the ironing would have been done with a *box iron*. This was a heavy metal box, tapering to a point at one end and with a small movable plate at the other end. Inside the box was a shaped piece of heavy stone or metal. This stone or metal would be placed in the open fire until it was hot enough, then transferred inside the box and kept in place by the movable plate which slotted in securely at the back of the iron.

Our toilet was outside in a privy in the back yard, with the water pipes lagged with sacking and a paraffin lamp hanging on them in winter – not for comfort but to stop the water in the pipes from freezing. Even so, there were many times when the ice in the bowl had to be broken before you could use the toilet. It was designed to keep visits short! At least, we didn't have to share the toilet with another family, as many people still had to do. No toilet rolls in those days, just sheets of paper torn from yesterday's *Daily Mirror*. Only people with ideas above their station cut the newspaper into squares. A few posh families may have used *Izal* toilet paper that was very hard and shiny on one side and not much different on the other. Soft toilet tissue was unknown then, certainly in our level of society.

When we moved into this house near the end of 1946, there was a corrugated steel *Anderson* air raid shelter half buried four feet deep in the ground in the back yard (not a garden). Originally the part above ground would have been covered with soil and sandbags as protection against bomb splinters. It looked very ugly and my mother soon persuaded my father to dig it out. This was not as easy as it sounds.

Since our house was owned by the firm where my father worked as foreman and it came with his job, my parents never had to worry about having the money for the weekly rent. In this, they were fortunate because in 1953, about six families in every ten lived in rented accommodation and two thirds of these rented from private landlords. Many families were often short of money and would send one of the children to the door when the rent man called to say the parents were out. Indeed, one of my friends remembers many occasions when he hid under the kitchen table with his mother and brother to avoid the rent man.

Poverty was much more widespread than today and even people who had regular jobs had only a few clothes - usually no more than one set of "Sunday best" for going to church or special occasions, one or maybe two regular outfits plus overalls for those whose job involved getting dirty. Patching clothes and darning woollen socks, pullovers and cardigans were very common. Women rarely went out of the house without a hat or headscarf. Many men, perhaps most, would wear a hat or cap and only civil servants or professional men carried an umbrella.

When the Second World War ended in 1945, every major city and town in Britain bore the scars of heavy bombing by the Luftwaffe. Bombed sites where once factories and houses had stood were scattered through the inner cities and were little more than piles of rubble. The clearing and development of these sites started shortly after the end of hostilities but proceeded much more slowly than planned. The last of these bombed sites remained until the end of the fifties or even into the sixties.

One project which did go ahead very quickly and successfully was the re-housing of peoples whose homes had been destroyed. Over a million houses were built between 1945 and 1951. Of these, over 150,000 were "prefabs"; temporary single storey houses built in factories and assembled on-site. These were intended to last for about ten years but several hundred of them were still being lived in at the start of the 21st century.

The early months of 1947 were exceptionally cold, with almost continuous snow from late January until March. The after effects of the Second World War on transport facilities did nothing to help, since most heavy goods, especially coal, were transported on trains. The railway system had been heavily bombed during the war and much remained to be repaired. Domestic and industrial supplies of electricity were cut, just as many people bought electric fires because of fears of a shortage of coal.

This winter, when I was three and a half, also provided me with the first personal experience that I can distinctly remember. I was playing one Sunday with my wooden train engine, a magnificent toy, about eighteen inches long, made for me by a family friend from County Down and painted in the green, black and red colours of the *Belfast & County Down Railway Company*. I was filling the tender with snow which lay thick in the front garage yard about twenty yards from the street, when my mother called me in for my tea. The main gates to the street were closed and locked but the smaller gate was not locked. After about twenty minutes I came out of the house to continue transporting this valuable cargo but the toy engine was gone, never to be seen again. I couldn't understand why the police were not interested in solving this major crime.

Primary School Days

I started infants' school in 1948, and my memories of it are limited to throwing beanbags, singing and playing the tambourine or triangle half a note after I should have. My most enduring memory of my time at the infants' school wasn't anything that happened in the classroom but of one afternoon when my class was sent home early because of a weather forecast promising a heavy thunderstorm. I ran the three hundred yards to my house and got home dry. Immediately behind the house was a flat waste ground where the buildings had been bombed during the War.

I can remember sitting at the table by the window in our living room, looking over this bombed site to the road I had just run up while I ate my slices of hot toast spread with butter and Bovril. There I was, dry and comfortable as I watched older children running in the now heavy rain, accompanied by the flashes of lighting and crashes of thunder. Maybe this memory of being warm and dry while watching the storm explains why, even to this day, I am fascinated by thunderstorms.

After about 18 months in the infants' school, I and a couple of other boys were kicked out to make room for younger children and so I started at "big school".

This was a fairly typical working class primary school of the time, less than two hundred yards from my house. The only slightly unusual things about it were that it was a Catholic school and for boys only. It wasn't particularly tough although you had to be able to stand up for yourself and there were a few people you walked carefully around. However, I enjoyed school and the games we played.

We sat at double desks which were built to last, with cast iron legs and wooden lids roughened by decades of boys carving grooves or scratching their names on the hinged lids. We would dig out the blotting paper stuffed into the inkwells and flick it at whoever had most recently annoyed us. Provided the blotting paper had been long enough in the inkwell to soak up most of the ink, it would come out as a semi-congealed lump of satisfyingly disgusting gunk, ideal as ammunition.

Another game was the *"splits"*. You would face another boy and each would throw their steel-tipped pens into the wooden floor at the outer side of their opponent's shoes. Wherever the pen stuck in the floor, you had to move your foot out to touch the pen. The object was to force the other boy to stand with his feet so far apart that he eventually lost his balance. But there was a strict rule. You had to throw the pen within a shoe's width of the outside of your opponent's shoe.

It was great fun but the effect on the pen nib didn't do much for your writing. If the aim was bad, it didn't do much for the shoes, either. Sometimes, the challenge was to use penknives, instead of pens. Whatever you thought about the possibility of a toe being amputated before you'd got to know it all that well, this was a challenge that could not be turned down – like all but the most foolhardy dares. So, you waited for the penknife to be thrown, wondering what you would say to your mother to explain the cut on the top of your shoe but nobody ever did lose a toe.

Every boy from about eight years old had a penknife. It was as essential as a pocketful of marbles and the pieces of string that were always going to come in useful someday. How could a boy whittle a piece of wood or make a bow and arrows without a penknife? The more expensive knives had various added tools like a tin-opener, a corkscrew and, strangest of all, a device for taking stones out of horses' hooves. I never knew anyone who had used this latter tool but most penknives had one. (This was in a much simpler time before we heard of, never mind saw, a Swiss Army knife.) But penknives were never used in fights. Fights were strictly fisticuff affairs and fought according to our own generally accepted ideas of fairness.

A catapult was another useful part of a boy's kit, preferably one he'd made himself out of a forked piece of wood from a small tree. Fitted with a piece of strong elastic which was threaded through a bit of bicycle inner tube, a boy could be David against Goliath, a commando silently attacking an enemy machine gun post at night or a hunter stalking the ginger tom from next door. In reality, the ginger tom was quite safe and sat six yards away, giving you a dirty look and openly sneering at your lack of skill.

Two other favourite games were marbles and conkers. Marbles were either coloured glass or clay, with glass ones worth about five clay ones. The clay marbles were definitely on the way out by the time I went to school and few people wanted to pit their glass marbles against clay ones.

The games varied from two players each putting an agreed number of marbles into a ring scored in the soil and taking turns to try to knock them out, to placing three, five or more marbles in a line touching each other on the ground and inviting your opponent to try and hit them from three, five or more paces and so win all the marbles. The trick here was to carefully position your line of marbles behind a slight and almost invisible bump in the playground surface, so that the bump would divert any marble that was rolled along the ground. This meant that your opponent could only hit your marbles by "dive bombing" them - a difficult thing to do. Every time he missed, you kept his marble. If he hit one of your marbles, he got the total number in the line.

An alternative, and very popular, game was to take it in turns to roll a marble along the street gutter, trying to hit the other person's marble as they leapfrogged past each other. The advantage of this was that you could play this game while walking home from school, even by yourself if necessary. In my case, although I lived only a short distance from the school, this game often slowed my progress homewards enough to get me told off by my mother for being late for my tea.

This particular game got me into more trouble than usual on one occasion when my mother sent me to get some eggs from the greengrocer's. I was about eight or nine at the time and a keen marble player. I bought the eggs and put them in a string bag (no shaped cardboard boxes to protect the eggs in those days!). On the way home I played gutter marbles, not noticing that every time I bent down to pick up a marble I also broke an egg. On the short journey home, I very efficiently broke every egg and possibly ended up without any tea at all that day.

The eggs and marbles incident is an example of how much we played in the street: marbles, cricket, football, various ball throwing games, hopscotch on the pavement (for girls), skipping, also for girls, unless you were a boxer, and many other games. Even if you weren't actually a boxer, you could rationalise skipping by pre-tending you were practising to take on Randolph Turpin, Sugar

Ray Robinson, Rocky Marciano or one of the other boxing Greats of the time. Of course, this only worked if you kept the skipping simple and did not do anything that girls did – like fancy twists and loops or skipping with the rope held by two girls standing five or six feet apart, or even skipping with *two* ropes. All these variations were looked upon by boys with scorn mainly, if truth were told, because boys could not compete successfully with the girls in these fancy add-ons to basic skipping.

Nor could boys compete with girls at hopscotch. This was essentially a balancing game which involved hopping on one foot and, using that same foot, kicking a piece of slate or stone completely into various squares without falling over. Boys always seemed to be too clumsy or too impatient to do this successfully. In any case, since boys had collectively decided that hopscotch was a *girl's* game and, therefore to be looked down upon, it was only in exceptional circumstances, where there were only one or two girls to play with, that a boy could be persuaded to join in – and then only if there no other boys about to witness this lapse from normal manly standards.

The various ball throwing games had one advantage over skipping and hopscotch. Boys could play them openly with girls – provided the boys won or, if they didn't, they thought quickly enough after losing and declared they had *let* the girls win out of a sense of chivalry! Needless to say, such a claim was loudly jeered by the girls. Away from the main roads, there were few cars to interrupt these games and when a car did come along, we simply stopped and waited until it had gone and carried on with our game.

Football and cricket were other popular street games because they were so easy to set up and someone always had a ball of some sort. All you needed then were two goals, easily provided by coats marking the goalposts or wickets chalked on walls or roughly scratched by a stone. A bat for cricket was easily found from the many pieces of wood in someone's back yard.

One thing which always puzzled us boys was that our mothers could not see how important it was to have your coats piled on the ground for the goals and that any mud which dirtied them was an unavoidable part of playing football. In fact, mothers seemed to have a totally unrealistic expectation that clothes were meant to be kept clean. Anyone who had a sense of what was right and proper knew they were actually intended for wiping sticky hands and providing carrying spaces for anything interesting which you had happened to pick up during your tours of inspection around the local area.

French cricket was another game which boys and girls could play together. The batter stood with both feet together and the aim of the other players was to hit his or her legs below the knee with the ball or to catch the ball when hit in the air. If the batter hit the ball to the side or even behind, the next ball came from where it had been fielded. You were not allowed to move your feet, so you had to twist yourself round and protect the side or the back of your legs with the bat. Most batting innings did not last very long, either because the batter couldn't easily defend the back of his or her legs, or because of claims that feet had been moved round against the rules.

Conkers (horse chestnuts) was a very popular game in autumn. There were strict rules as to what you could do to harden your conker. If you baked the conker or pickled it, or if it was last year's model (and so harder than fresh ones) or even two years old, you had to tell your opponent but only if asked. You kept a count of how many victories each conker had won and if your *sixer* broke a rival's *twoer* or *fourer*, your conker became an *eighter* or *tenner* and so on.

One year I was given a bag of conkers by an older friend. They had been lying in his house for five or more years and so were rock hard. No-one thought of checking conkers back that far. So, I had a set of invincible conkers but, by the time I had got *a hundred and ninety-sixer*, I was fed up with all the easy wins. I destroyed all my champions by throwing them against the wall of my house.

At about the same time that I started primary school, my mother gave birth to my younger brother, Stephen. In 1950 it was the custom for the nurses to give each new mother a daily bottle of Guinness to build up their strength after the birth. After the first bottle, my mother refused to have any more.

A couple of months later, while she made a quick trip to the greengrocer's, only a hundred yards away, my mother left me in charge of my brother who was lying in his big pram and, as he was unable to do anything but lie there, he was not strapped in. I took it into my head to inspect my charge and, standing at the bottom of the pram with my arms over the handle, peered in. Unfortunately, I tilted the pram up to see better and my brother slid gently out of the bottom of the pram and onto the floor.

He was not hurt but I soon found that he was too heavy for me to pick up and put back in the pram. My solution was to roll him up the side of the pram and tip him in. Of course, he didn't take kindly to this and started complaining loudly. As he cried, I cried as well so that, when my mother came back after about five minutes, she was met with the sound of two sons crying for all they were worth. I was not left in charge of my brother again for a long time.

A Letter To The Headmaster

Discipline in my primary school was fairly strict but not harsh. We accepted that you got a ruler or gym shoe across the hand for misbehaving in class but only the headmaster and his deputy used the cane. On one occasion, when I was about ten, we were being taught arithmetic in a classroom with tall, narrow church-like windows and a wide window ledge along one wall. Those of us who sat beside this wall had a game when one particular teacher was trying to drive some knowledge of maths into our heads.

While the teacher was writing on the blackboard, we would sit up on the window ledge and the winner was the last person to sit down without being caught when the teacher turned round again to face the class. On this occasion, I sat down first out of the five or six boys in the game and had the humiliation of being definitely the loser in that round. I was determined to be the first to sit up on the ledge at the next opportunity when the teacher faced the black-board. So, when it came, I shot up like a rocket, so fast that my backside broke the window and I nearly followed the broken glass out onto the playground outside.

Of course, I was sent for punishment to the headmaster. This particular gentleman was very keen on sports, especially boxing. I was not interested in boxing but, if you were good at any sport, you could get into his good books. I was the fastest runner in the school so, instead of getting the cane, I got away with a good telling off. As I lived so close to the school, I used to go home for lunch. When I arrived home, I don't know if I looked guilty, or if my (short) trousers were torn but my mother got the whole story out of me and she was furious.

I got a letter to take back to the headmaster effectively asking what kind of a school he was running where a boy could mess around in class, break a window and not get punished! Needless to say, I got six of the cane on the guilty backside. I wonder if there would be the same reaction from a parent today? Whatever the answer might be nowadays, in the fifties, if you got into trouble at school, you got into at least as much trouble again when you arrived home. The funny thing was, the sitting up on the window ledge game didn't seem just so attractive after that.

Fights were fairly common, usually short bouts broken up in the playground by a teacher but occasionally an insult was given which could only be avenged by more formal combat. One such insult I received could only be wiped out by a duel at the OK Corral, or our local equivalent – that is, on the footpath outside the school gate, at four o'clock.

Surrounded by a crowd of classmates shouting encouragement, my insulter and I scrapped under (more or less) Marquis of Queensbury Rules until a teacher came out of the school and we were separated and sent home. I got a black eye – enough to get me into trouble with my mother (but not at all with my father) but I was happy and could claim a victory on points. You see, I had knocked out two of my rival's teeth! (They were probably the last of his first teeth and due to fall out soon anyway but that is not how I thought at the time).

By the way, on several occasions when one of my first teeth was loose and close to falling out, I would try to dislodge it completely by pushing at it with my tongue. If that didn't work, my mother would tie a piece of thread around the loose tooth and give a sharp pull which usually got the tooth out without too much pain. Other people's mothers would sometimes tie the free end of the thread to a door handle and then slam the door shut, giving the same result but a bit more painfully as the thread or string attached to the door handle was horizontal, whereas, if your mother did the pulling she could pull downwards and so cause less pain.

Another thing which comes to mind from my time in primary school was the school radio. Programmes were relayed from the receiver in the headmaster's office to the portable loudspeaker brought into the classroom. These programmes included geography and nature programmes but I remember especially the music programmes we had every week. Songs to which we were introduced included: *"Were you ever in Quebec? (stowing timber on the deck)"*, *"Away boys, away, (for we're bound for the Rio Grande)"* and *"Alouette, gentille alouette"*, all of which were fine, manly songs, the last one being a song of the *voyageurs*, the French trappers in 18th century Canada who would sing it to help them keep time as they paddled their canoes loaded with furs and skins back to the trading posts where they would sell them

So, while we were singing such songs, we could easily imagine ourselves as tough sailors on board sailing ships rounding Cape Horn, or equally tough hunters braving the dangers of the Canadian wilderness. Unfortunately, we also had to sing the Hansel and Gretel song from Humperdinck's opera (*"Brother, come and dance with me, both my hands I offer thee"*) and *"Lavender's blue dilly, dilly, lavender's green, when I am King dilly, dilly, you shall be my Queen"*. These were anything but manly songs but we still had to sing them under the watchful gaze of Miss Hazelwood, our kindly but still strict class teacher.

Miss Hazlewood gave us weekly tests in multiplication and we had to prove we had learned our tables up to times twelve. Our exercise books had these tables printed on the back cover, together with tables of distance – *inches, feet, yards, poles perches or roods, chains, furlongs* and *miles*. For some reason, poles, perches and *roods* (the last not to be confused with *roods*, a measure of area but they always were) always gave me trouble. Then, there were *statute* miles, *Scottish* miles. *nautical* miles and even *Irish* miles, each of them longer than the previous one.

Weights were listed in ascending order; *grains, pennyweights, ounces, pounds, stones, quarters, hundredweights and tons*. When it came to measures of volume, these depended on whether you were dealing in dry goods – *pecks* and *bushels*, or in liquids - *gills, pints, quarts* and *gallons*. And this is not even bringing *firkins* or *kilderkins* into consideration. After all these, it was a relief to get back to something simple like *farthings, ha'pennies* (pronounced *"haypennies"), pennies, thruppenny bits, sixpences, shillings, florins, half crowns, ten shilling notes* and *pound notes*. (*Fivers* and higher value notes were things we may have read about in fiction but we had never seen any.)

Government Health Measures

Another thing I remember throughout my school years was the free third of a pint (about 180 ml) of milk we got each morning – a Government initiative aimed at improving the health of children who were still affected by rationing and food shortages after the end of the Second World War. (Wartime and post-war rationing was actually very carefully worked out and led to a much better balanced and healthier diet than most children had before the War – or indeed since, as there were few sweets or biscuits to be had.)

During cold weather –and there was a lot of that – the milk crate would be placed in the hearth of the open coal fire which was the only heating in our classroom. This unfroze the milk but also gave you a semi warm drink which made you gag when it was left too long by the fire. By the way, did you know that twelve third-of-a-pint bottles of milk, drunk very quickly, can make you feel drunk? At least, that was how it seemed to me at the end of a milk-drinking contest.

In addition to state-supplied milk, many other initiatives were introduced by the Labour Government to improve the health of the young. Concentrated orange juice in a medicine bottle was supplied to children. This was so strong that it had to be heavily diluted to make it palatable. No such luck with the cod liver oil, a tablespoonful of which was the dose from my mother every morning, followed by a bit of dry bread dipped in salt to take the taste away. There weren't any taste-free capsules then. Regular winter "treats" also included *Minadex* - a general tonic which was green and *Scott's Emulsion* which was white and reminded my taste buds unpleasantly of a mixture of water, chalk and fish oil.

To avoid upsetting the manufacturers of these tonics, I should point out that my range of acceptable tastes was very limited at that time and, in any case, both products have probably seen many improvements since the days when I pulled a face at the thought of having to take them. Another remedy favoured by my mother for myself and later for my younger brother was *California Syrup of Figs* to keep us "regular" (a very important concept then). Why the figs were Californian was something I never understood.

The one tonic which I really *did* forward to getting was *"Virol"* a vitamin preparation based on malt extract. To me, it was like getting a big spoonful of soft toffee and, thirty years after I had enjoyed getting my daily spoonful, I couldn't understand why all my children turned up their noses at it. Can you still get it now?

Owing to the universal use of coal both for domestic heating and industrial use, the air in cities in the 1950s was much less clean than nowadays. This led to various chest and breathing problems among children and adults. A very common way of treating the complaints (and one endorsed by many doctors) was to take the child to the local gasworks and to have them breath in the air around the works for a quarter or half an hour. The relatively high proportion of town gas in the air around the gasworks was supposed to have a beneficial effect but I don't know if it did.

Local Shops

Mention of bread as an antidote to the taste of cod liver oil turns my mind to the foods we ate and the shops which supplied them. Supermarkets were unknown and most people bought their groceries from small shops converted from the front room of a house, or from the Co-op. There was no Co-op near us, so we did our ordinary shopping in Mr Godwin's grocery shop a few doors away from our house.

The shop was no more than the front room of an ordinary "Coronation Street" style house, about twelve feet square, with a counter dividing it in two. If three people were waiting to be served, the shop was crowded. Compared to Mr Godwin's, the shop depicted in Ronnie Barker's 1970s TV comedy *"Open all hours"* was a veritable emporium. Mr Godwin would bring out a side of bacon from its place in the coolest part of the house for de-boning with a ferociously long knife, cut it into manageable pieces which he would proceed to slice to a customer's order on a magnificent but dangerous-looking hand-operated bacon slicer with a gleaming circular "saw" which could adjusted for different thicknesses of rashers.

Like the bacon, hardly anything was pre-packed. Butter was cut and weighed to order from a huge block behind the counter and handed over in greaseproof paper. Cheese, too, was cut with a thin wire from a block wrapped in cheesecloth, so you could get half a pound or two ounces as required, sugar was weighed out from big sacks into strong paper bags. You could still find shops where tea was also scooped out from large tea chests into a paper bag and weighed out, like everything else, on a big set of scales.

The scales had a flat plate on one side where brass weights from half an ounce up to two pounds were placed, while the other side had a pan into which whatever was being weighed was placed. Weights were added or taken away until both sides of the scale balanced at the correct amount. Our butcher, on the other hand was either very go-ahead (he was considerably younger than Mr Godwin), or not very good at mental arithmetic, or he was a soft touch for equipment salesmen, for he had a modern, spring-balanced scales. This was quicker to use than the older type because it had a bewildering (to a young customer) set of prices printed on it, which made instant calculation of the price possible.

Of course, this was long before electronic weighing scales which also calculate the price, so this was just one example of how shopkeepers in the fifties constantly had to use their brains in their work and not rely on electronic assistance. If they weren't confident about their ability in mental arithmetic, a pencil (usually kept behind the ear, like a spare cigarette) and piece of paper were always available.

Biscuits came in large tin boxes, sometimes with a glass lid so you could see what was on offer, again to be weighed out to order. The best value were the assorted broken biscuits, sold at cut price, and best of all was when you got broken chocolate biscuits in the mixture. Many sweets were in glass bottles and you always watched hopefully when getting one or two pennyworth to see if you would get an extra sweet to take the pointer on the weighing scale over the line marking the correct weight. A grocer who tossed an extra sweet or two on the scales was never short of small boys and girls as customers.

Among our favourite sweets were *blackjacks* – square hard liquorice toffees, aniseed balls, (both of which were ten for a penny) - and *gobstoppers* - balls of flavour which got their name because when a nine year old had one of these, it effectively filled the mouth and stopped you doing anything else, like talking. Of course, when you were nine, you just had to see if you could swallow one of these gobstoppers whole. This was not advisable because, not only did you lose the entire sweet in one swallow which was a waste as it was ten times the price of a blackjack, it also nearly choked you. Another favourite could only be found in a small sweet shop in the next street. *Gongers* or *cinder chocolate* were irregular shaped lumps of honeycomb sugar centre, similar to *Crunchie* bars but more roughly made. These were on a stick like an ice lolly. This sweet shop was also where I got my first taste of sherbert filled *flying saucers*.

Much of the bread sold in Mr Godwin's shop was unsliced and unwrapped and using tongs or putting on disposable gloves before handling the loaves (or anything else unwrapped) was unknown. No doubt, the hygiene in most shops was almost non-existent by today's standards and germs were readily transferred from one item to another but we certainly built up an immunity to many of these germs and common modern day ailments like allergies were rare – or, at least, rarely recognised.

There were very few refrigerators or domestic freezers in the 1950s so perishable foods were bought in small quantities every day or every few days. Boiled ham would be bought in amounts of a quarter pound, or less, and meat and fish would be bought on the day it was to be used. The meat might be stretched for a second day – or even a third if it contained a bone which could be used for a broth or stew. Our milk was delivered every morning and, as we had pasteurised milk, in hot weather the bottles would be placed in a big saucepan of cold water and, if it was very hot, a teacloth over the bottles and dipping into the water to encourage evaporation and cool the milk. My mother did not like sterilised milk, although it was the more popular type in Birmingham (unlike most of the rest of the country). This could be left unopened indefinitely but had to be used quickly once it was opened.

The empty milk bottles were collected by the milkman next day, cleaned and re-used several times. This recycling of glass was very common. Pop or lemonade bottles had a deposit of two or three pence charged on them and this deposit could be reclaimed when the empty bottles were returned to the shop. Small boys were always on the lookout for empty lemonade bottles lying about which could be collected up and used to generate extra pocket money.

Up until the early fifties, some foods were still rationed due to the after effects of the War. Sweets and sugar were rationed until 1953 and food rationing did not completely end until 1954. I can just about remember taking the family's ration book to Mr Godwin's grocery and getting a certain number of coupons cut out in order to buy sweets. While rationing was in force, people had to register with a particular grocer or butcher. This gave rise to a thriving illegal black market for people who had money and ample opportunities for *spivs* (black marketeers) - perhaps best illustrated by Private Walker in the television comedy *Dad's Army* - who seemed to be able to get supplies of anything which was in short supply, for a price. It was hard for people to resist getting involved in the black market, either for the few luxuries which were available for those who had money to spare or, more usually, to buy extra sugar or butter or something which the shopkeeper kept "under the counter" for a special family event or a favoured customer.

Cigarettes and Cigarette Cards

Smoking was very common and in any group of men (except at church) you could not avoid breathing in second hand smoke. Most men and many women smoked. And many people started smoking at a young age. My father smoked heavily, forty cigarettes a day for many years, and he gave me one of his Players Navy Cut "medium strength" cigarettes when I was about eight or nine. He made sure I nearly finished it. Although I did not actually get sick, I felt so ill that I never wanted to smoke another cigarette until I was eighteen and started going out with a slightly older girl who smoked, when I became a light smoker for a few years.

Many of the cigarettes brands of that time have disappeared, although some remain. Player's Navy Cut, with a picture of a sailor and a battleship, HMS Hero, on the packet, was one of the most popular brands, together with Will's Woodbine. The latter was a more down market brand than Player's and many grocers sold Woodbines in open paper packets of five or even in ones or twos on Thursdays, when a customer was waiting for his wages on a Friday. Other popular brands were Will's Gold Flake, Player's Weights, Capstan, Craven "A", Park Drive, State Express, Senior Service, Pall Mall and Kensitas. My father liked to get Carroll's or Gallaher's (both Irish brands) when he could.

Cigarette packets were very popular among young boys who would pick up any found thrown away. But not the flip top packets which were beginning to come into fashion. We would flatten the ordinary outer packets (20s were by far the best) and skim them in competition with other boys. The object of the game was either to see how far you could skim the packet or to cover your opponent's packet with your own and so take it over to add to your collection.

Games

By the fifties, cigarette cards were no longer included in the packets as they had been in the 1940s and earlier but they were still to be found in packets of sweet cigarettes. These were popular, not so much for their taste but because, with one of these "cigarettes" in between your lips or behind your ear, you could easily be *Dick Barton, Special Agent*, a daring ace pilot, a *"cop"* or a *"robber"*, or a Western sheriff to be feared by any outlaws who might ride into the neighbourhood. In my case, my ears stuck out just too much to hold one of these "cigarettes" firmly in place.

Cops and Robbers and Cowboys and Indians were two of the favourites games for boys and most days there would be gunfights with the participants shooting (always accurately, of course) from behind makeshift barricades or peering around corners. Occasionally, girls would be tolerated in these games but usually only as hostages or as victims to be rescued from Red Indians intent on burning them at the stake. Sometimes there would be a tomboy in the group who insisted on being Calamity Jane and usually played the role very effectively. Water pistols (for Cops and Robbers) and cap pistols (for Cowboys and Indians) made things more realistic – at least in our minds.

Even more realistic, especially when we were re-fighting the Second World War or saving the world from evil enemy spies, were the "authentic" plastic *Luger* automatic pistol, preferably "liberated" (we knew all the technical terms) from a captured enemy agent, and a *potato gun*. This last had a small tube sticking out of the front of the barrel. You pulled back a lever, which compressed a spring in the barrel, then you pushed the barrel into an apple or raw potato to fill the tube. Then when you pulled on the trigger, the spring was released, expanded and fired the apple or potato "ammunition" at your target. The Luger's ammunition was a lightweight plastic pellet. These two guns could give a sharp pain to your enemy if your aim was good, so were not encouraged by mothers and aiming at the face was expressly forbidden.

"Pirates" was also a popular game and many a younger brother was forced to walk the plank into shark-infested waters. This particular game gave plenty of scope for sword fighting with swords made from odd pieces of wood, finding buried treasure and performing other examples of derring-do on imaginary tropical seas and islands.

As *Tarzan* films were still very popular, jungle hideaways abounded. There weren't any trees or bushes in our back yard so my friends and I couldn't make a tree house and we were forced to make do with an old upturned table with old sheets and towels draped over the legs and down the sides. The lack of any kind of tree meant that I could not practise swinging from branch to branch on ropes – a major drawback when you were supposed to be Tarzan. Our cat was enlisted to act as a lion or tiger but it never seemed to be too enthusiastic about its role and usually soon wandered off in disgust. Nor did we have anyone to take the part of Maureen O'Sullivan as Jane but we still managed to beat our scrawny chests and utter blood curdling jungle cries.

More Shops

One of the reasons I was happy to go regularly to Mr Godwin's for groceries, or "messages" as my mother called them with her northern Irish upbringing, was that he sometimes asked me to go to the local wholesaler for small items which had run out of stock. The wholesaler was only about half a mile away. While I waited for the order to be made up, I would wander around, completely unsupervised (we hadn't heard of "Health and Safety" then), among the shelves and stacks of goods from all sorts of *faraway places with strange sounding names* as a popular Bing Crosby song described them. I was fascinated by names such as the Gold Coast, Trinidad, Santiago, Ceylon, Zanzibar, Tanganyika, California, and so on. The smells coming from the sacks of coffee or spices, or open tea chests, and many other exotic smells (exotic to me, at least) were a source of wonder and delight and perhaps started off a wanderlust which would later have an important bearing on the course of my life.

The two other most important regular shopping points were the local greengrocer and the local butcher but, from the point of view of an eight to ten year old, neither had the attraction of the workers' café at the end of the road. I would sometimes be sent here to get a sandwich or something for the mechanics who worked with my father in the garage beside our house.

Thick slices of toast covered with butter were popular or, best of all, bread with beef dripping spread thickly. The men would tear off a corner of the greaseproof bag and hold their "piece" with it to prevent the car grease on their hands getting on it. I used to be fascinated by this and, whenever one of the men offered me a slice, I would also tear off a corner of the bag and hold my piece in the same way and consider myself at least the equal of any other man there. A strange fact was that the toast or dripping piece bought in that café always tasted better than ones made at home, even if the home-made ones were toasted on a long fork in front of the fire. Low fat spreads would have been against these mechanics' religion – even if they had been thought of in the fifties.

One of the main differences between the local areas in the 40s, 50s and early 60s and "neighbourhoods" today was that you could find every kind of shop for all your everyday needs within a ten minute walk for an adult - twenty minutes or half an hour, if you were a young boy. This time discrepancy was because there was always something to attract your interest as you walked along and you would have to stop and watch it for a while, even though you had strict instructions from your mother to hurry back with whatever you had been sent to get! Grocers, greengrocers, butchers, news-agents, chemist, post office, laundry, drapery, cinema, hardware, barbers (short back and sides every fortnight was the normal schoolboy cut). All these businesses were small and locally owned except, perhaps, the cinema.

By the mid-fifties, we even had a *"Continental"* shop, selling strange new foods like okra and sweet potatoes, tinned octopus, French coffee, salami, olive oil and so on. But the things which fascinated me most as I gazed at the exotic items displayed in the shop window were the small packets of chocolate covered ants, looking just like the packets of chocolate covered sultanas and peanuts you could buy in ordinary shops. I never did have the courage to try the ants which were, according to the wording on the packet, both "delicious and "nutritious" but I did often wonder what they tasted like. Oddly enough, I recently read about a UN report which recommends we should eat insects like ants and grasshoppers as part of a healthy diet because they provide more protein by weight than conventional foods like beef. The report did not specify if the insects are "delicious" as well as "nutritious".

Our local greengrocer used to sell rabbits. Rabbit pie and stews were very popular. The rabbits for sale would be half skinned and hung on steel hooks, without any refrigeration. The popularity of rabbits as meat suddenly stopped in 1953 when myxomatosis spread to England. The newspapers were full of pictures of dying or dead wild rabbits with horribly swollen heads and these pictures effectively put an end to the rabbit trade.

The range of vegetables and fruit sold in our local greengrocers shop was much smaller than today. Potatoes (usually King Edwards), carrots, turnips, cabbage, cauliflower, Brussels sprouts, celery, broad beans, peas (fresh, in their pods), tomatoes, apples, pears, strawberries, raspberries, plums, peaches and rhubarb comprised most of what was on offer.

All of these were products grown in season in the countryside surrounding the towns of the West Midlands or, at least, grown in Britain. New potatoes from the Channel Islands or Cyprus were a rarity. Bananas were a treat and mandarins and dates only available at Christmas. If you wanted blackberries or mushrooms, you could go into the nearest piece of countryside and pick them yourself. Different fruits and vegetables were only available during their season – all year round availability of all fruits and vegetables was unknown, except possibly to a small number of well-off people living in exclusive areas of London and the Southeast of England.

Unlike today, when you can go to any city or town and see the same supermarkets and shops in the High Street or, more likely the huge Shopping Centre, in the fifties almost the only shops with such nation-wide presence were a few department stores, the Co-op and Woolworths and Lewis's in the Midlands and North of England. Most of these had not yet modernised and a Sleeping Beauty who had fallen asleep in 1933 could have walked into any of them in 1953 and seen few changes.

I remember going into (I think) Woolworth's with my mother sometime about 1953. I have no idea what she bought but I remember being fascinated by the way her payment for the item was placed in a little tube which was hung on to a moving wire system attached to the ceiling which transferred it to a central cash area. Here the payment was checked, a receipt and change placed back in the tube and the lot travelled back to where my mother was waiting. The web of wires was like a miniaturised railway system with its point changes taking tubes to their various destinations.

Christmas is Coming

After the conker season was over and the nights were drawing in, it was not long before thoughts started to turn towards Christmas.

Halloween would pass largely un-noticed except in Irish or Scottish families where it revolved around ghost stories, apples and nuts and not the artificial, Americanised "spookiness" that children are used to today. Guy Fawkes Night followed and was much more widely celebrated, with bonfires, Catherine Wheels, bangers and rockets launched from empty milk bottles. Old furniture and rubbish would have been collected for days or weeks for a bonfire. Many younger brothers (or sisters) would have to put up with being dressed in old clothes, their faces blackened with soot and being paraded in an old pram while their older brothers collected "*a penny for the Guy*". As far as I know, all these "guys" were replaced by one made of old clothes before it was time to actually place them on a bonfire!

Unlike now, shops did not start the Christmas promotions until nearly the end of November but from then on, a small boy or girl's impatience would grow. Pennies and thruppeny bits would be saved in preparation for buying presents for your mother and father and, when you'd saved just enough for them, you realised that you'd better get something for your little brother. The choice of this present was the most difficult because it was very hard to find something you could afford which you could plausibly give to someone seven years younger than you and still be able to play with it yourself. Eventually, two or three days before Christmas, the decorations would be taken out of their boxes and hung up. The Christmas tree would be ordered for collection on Christmas Eve. During the last few days before Christmas, our kitchen would be filled with the smells of baking because my mother did not believe in baking cakes and puddings weeks before.

Christmas Eve arrived. This was usually a time of rushing to the shops for something forgotten, or something which had to be bought fresh. All this was done by mothers and children because most fathers worked on Christmas Eve, perhaps getting off from work a couple of hours early. The Christmas milk and *cream* (a very rare treat) was delivered late on Christmas Eve. Postmen delivered cards twice on Christmas Eve and once on Christmas morning.

Over a period of a few days before Christmas, the milkman, postman, dustbin men and others would knock at the front door to wish *"Compliments of the Season"* and to collect their Christmas box. Incidentally, the bin men seemed miraculously to have been able to collect the rubbish for two weeks before Christmas without leaving a selection of it on the ground outside the front gate where it had to be cleaned up by the housewives of the street. Once the rubbish collections started again in the New Year, this spurt of tidiness evaporated, especially at houses where the *"Compliments of the Season"* had not been answered with a little drinking money.

Mr Godwin's shop, like many other small grocer's, butcher's and greengrocer's, opened for a couple of hours on Christmas morning before Christmas dinner to allow last minute purchases of some forgotten essential, such as *Bisto*. Buses in Birmingham ran from nine, or so, in the morning to about one o'clock to allow people get to and from religious services.

But, back to Christmas Eve. A good wash, clean clothes and shoes, a lie down in the early evening because tonight, the first event of Christmas was Midnight Mass. Arriving back home about an hour or so after midnight, it was upstairs, a sock hung up on the bed, and eventually sleep. Up again after about four or five hour's sleep, a rub of the eyes and what had Santa brought? Well, he always filled the sock which now lay on the top of the bed clothes. That was the first thing to inspect. There were no surprises. There was always an apple and a mandarin, some sweets, a coin and maybe a puzzle. But wait! There *is* a surprise – the coin is, in fact, a *shilling piece* (5p). Wealth beyond the dreams of avarice!

Now up out of bed to see what else had arrived silently during the night. Always a book or two, very welcome as I was a keen reader, and a game – maybe blow football or a pinball game. Into my parents' bedroom *"Mammy, Daddy". Look what I've got"*. These were in addition to the present from my parents waiting downstairs under the Christmas tree. One year, this turned out to be a clockwork train set, another year a *Meccano* set which was welcomed by my father as much as by me.

Back to bed but not to sleep. This is a really exciting book! Shooting the metal balls of the pinball game and just missing the highest score before finally being claimed for a while by sleep. Then, downstairs where the fire was already lit. Breakfast first, then putting the railway tracks together and starting the express on its journey. Where will I put the tunnel?

Other welcome presents included a Viewmaster 3D viewer with its circular series of pairs of pictures which would give realistic (to our minds, anyway) three dimensional views of lions leaping out at you in the plains of Africa or images of brightly coloured tropical birds. Another useful present was a *Dan Dare* film strip projector shaped like a ray gun which allowed you to see one of the famous space hero's battles with the *Mekon* projected on to a wall in a darkened room.

Very rarely, there might be a more expensive toy like a *Scalextric* car racing game or the *Meccano* set I mentioned above. This was the present of presents. In order to get one you had to have reached the ripe old age of nine or so – there were none of those suspect plastic versions like nowadays. This was the *real* metal thing with tiny brass nuts and bolts unsuited for less mature fingers. However, there was one drawback in getting a *Meccano* set. You had always to be on the alert against a parental takeover bid because fathers had a tendency to want to help you or show you how to do things properly and, if you weren't careful, you could soon find yourself as a spectator instead of an inventor.

Other toys which were gratefully received were sets of *Dinky* toys. Like most young boys in those days, I thought these were for racing or for crashing into each other, not realising that they were intended to be kept in pristine condition, preferably with their box intact, and to be sold decades later for tens, hundreds or, even in some cases, thousands of pounds!

Before you realised it, it was time to get ready for Christmas dinner. From the kitchen came the gorgeous smells of the cooking ham and beef (my parents were not all that keen on turkey), roast potatoes and Yorkshire pudding and the less gorgeous smells of Brussels sprouts and cabbage. The homemade Christmas pudding was having its final steaming in the big saucepan. Every year I would pester my mother to make a round Christmas pudding, like the ones enjoyed by Korky the Cat, Biffo the Bear and all the other characters in the various comics but it always appeared pudding bowl shaped. At last everything was ready and the food was brought to the table. My father carved the meat, my mother poured the gravy over everything on the plate and then we said Grace, *"Bless us O Lord and these Thy gifts which we are about to receive from Thy bounty, through Christ, Our Lord. Amen."* And so we ate Christmas dinner, followed by a generous helping of Christmas pudding and custard.

After dinner, my father sometimes had a bottle of Guinness and the afternoon went on quietly, maybe with the wireless turned on to the *Light Programme* and me enjoying my new presents until I started teasing my younger brother, or he annoyed me. Then, it was time to have a slice of Christmas cake and to get ready to visit my parents' friends, the Cooks, for the evening. We would leave our house about six o'clock and walk the half mile or so and then enter another world.

There were two brothers, Jack and Arthur, and a sister, Teresa – all unmarried and all a few years older than my parents. Jack, always known to my brother and myself as "Mr Cook" - was a toolmaker in an engineering factory and the lead tenor in our church choir, as well as being my father's best friend. As soon as we stepped into the house, the 1950s disappeared and we were in the 1930s, or even 20s. The table would be laden with cold meats, breads, trifle and Christmas cake. Mince pies would be waiting on the sideboard. The meal would start and proceed leisurely. My father and the two brothers would have a drop of whisky and then a bottle of beer, or two. Teresa Cook would have a glass of sherry, and my mother would have a tomato juice or pineapple juice while my brother and I would have *Tizer* or *American Cream Soda*.

After the meal, time would shift back further again and we would be entertained to an Edwardian evening of ghost stories, magic tricks, which I could never work out, and songs which were always unaccompanied. My mother would be prevailed on to sing *"The Mountains of Mourne"*, *"October winds lament around the Castle of Dromore"*, *"Danny Boy"*, or some other traditional Irish air. I would have to do a party piece which was always an embarrassment but at least I could usually get away with a humorous poem.

However, Mr Cook would provide most of the singing, standing by the mantelpiece of the open coal fire, mixing Irish songs from John McCormack and Josef Locke with traditional English songs like *"The Floral Dance"* and *"The Lincolnshire Poacher"* and always finishing up with *"Bless this House, O Lord, we pray, keep it safe by night and day"* and *"The Holy City"* (*"Jerusalem, Jerusalem, Lift up your gates and sing Hosannas in the highest to your Saviour and your*

King"). Then it was time to walk the short distance home, with my brother almost asleep on my father's back.

I intended to spend some time in bed reading or playing with the pinball game when we got home but sleep always had other ideas.

Memories of A Country Childhood

Playing in the garden which always seemed to be in bloom,
Making my own garden, bordered with London Pride.
Swinging on the swing, at the side of the house.

Riding my tricycle down the path then racing around the house to climb the front door and clinging on for dear life to the letter box. Who was after me? Oh! Her name was Patsy, She was only a pup!

Going for a walks in the country with my mother and sisters.
We could collect anything in their due season -
bluebells, blackberries, strawberries, hazelnuts and conkers from the last of which we would get great sport.

Sitting in the Piggery with my Father, watching him look after the animals and sometimes getting the odd ride down the lane on the back of a pig.
The rooster which used to chase us around the yard.

Sliding down the big sandpit beside our house and watching the sand martins diving into their small holes in the sandbanks. Making mud pies for hours and hours.

Waiting patiently for a sign of Mammy and Daddy coming home from the shopping trip in Kidderminster every Thursday with our weekly ration of sweets - pieces of rock, macaroons - they came in all shapes.

My big sister Anne's sixth birthday party when she got two satchels and was persuaded to give me one. How grown up I felt with my new satchel, going to catch the bus for my first day at school. I remember the dragonflies that used to block our path on our way down the lane.

The lovely bonfires, the fireworks, especially the Catherine Wheels nailed on a post and whizzing round and round to make a spinning stream of light and sparks and the lovely roast chestnuts and the potatoes cooked in the ashes of the fire

The walks in our Sunday clothes to Church, the lighting of the gas lamps with a taper, the passing around of hymn and prayer books and the singing of old traditional hymns.

Then, the Sunday afternoon walks with my sisters to our two Aunties' houses and the lovely buns made especially for us every week by my Aunty Lily.

I can smell & taste them yet.

The friends I had in years gone, playing in grounds of the Stewpony Hotel and Stourton Castle. Watching the house boats on the canal, Listening to folk tell old stories about the Gibbet Wood, close to our house and the Highwaymen who had been hanged there long, long ago

There are many more memories.
So I thank my Mother and Father for all of these
And for the freedom we had to play and explore our environment in good times and times which were sometimes not so good – but always filled with love.

Rosemary

Summer Holidays

Most people took their two week summer holidays at roughly the same time, between the middle of July and the middle of August. In many towns, whole industries closed down for the last week in July and the first in August. Many people stayed at home or went for day trips into the seaside or countryside. Towards the end of the 1950s a few people flew to Spain on one of the recently introduced *"package holidays"*. But most people who could afford to get away for a while spent their week or two weeks in one of the many seaside holiday resorts like Blackpool, Scarborough, Skegness, or Bridlington, if they lived in the North of England; Rhyl, Llandudno, or Weston Super Mare, if they lived in the Midlands; or Brighton, Clacton, Southend, or Great Yarmouth, if they lived in the London area. Wealthier professional people might spend their holiday in more "genteel" places like Eastbourne, Frinton or Bognor Regis.

In the main resorts, like Blackpool, accommodation ranged from hotels of various standards to guesthouses and boarding houses. Boarding house landladies were the stock targets of many comedians who would joke about their strictness: doors locked at a certain time at night, rigid mealtimes, sub-standard food, negative attitude towards guests who drank alcohol, and so on. However, many provided a high standard of service when compared to what people were used to in their own home and I suppose most landladies fell in between these two extremes. The proof that most landladies were not like the comedians claimed was shown by the fact that many families went back, year after year, to the same boarding house.

Most big resorts had one or more piers and all types of amusements: shooting galleries with rifles which never seemed to shoot where you aimed them, coconut shies – (where the suspicion was that the coconuts were glued into the holders so that they were almost impossible to dislodge even if you hit them), quoits, fortune tellers, donkey rides, Punch and Judy shows, photographers ready to take your picture with your wife or girlfriend, husband or boyfriend (remember, this was a time when most people did not have many photos and, probably, not even a camera), dance halls and theatres. Dodgem cars, roller coasters and helter-skelters, sandcastles, candy floss, sticks of rock (how *did* they get the resort's name printed all through the rock?) and the illuminations – all these were part of the annual holiday for millions of people. Most of the great comics and singers of the time would do a summer season at these resorts – Arthur Askey, Tommy Cooper, Morecambe and Wise, Josef Locke, Ken Dodd, Winifred Atwell, Max Bygraves and many, many more.

Holiday camps were also at the height of their popularity in the 1950s. Butlin's, Pontin's and Warner's were the leaders, with camps all around the coast. Variety shows and talent shows led many people to stardom, among them Des O'Connor, Dave Allen, Jimmy Tarbuck. The camps were meant to provide everything a holidaymaker could want, so there would be no need for them to venture outside. Ballrooms, swimming pools and facilities for all sorts of games and talent and beauty contests, even a chapel at some places, meant that people could, if they wanted, spend their entire holiday without setting foot outside the camp.

My Holidays – Trains and Ships

My own summer holidays were very different. Every year, during the school summer holiday, my mother and I, together with my younger brother, would travel to stay for a month or more with my grandparents in County Down. My father would follow later, when he had his two weeks off in August. This was a most exciting time because we got to travel on an express train and a big ship which, in my young opinion was at least comparable to the famous Atlantic liners like the Queen Elizabeth and Queen Mary! What better start could you have to a holiday? The experience was totally different from travelling from today's airports and much more adventurous, even if just as crowded.

Our journey started from either British Railways' London Midland region's New Street Station or the Western region's Snow Hill Station. These, like many of the big city stations, were huge buildings with glass roofs, made grimy by the smoke from over ninety years of steam locomotives, and long platforms. Both stations were very draughty and, as far as I remember, both had separate waiting rooms for men and ladies (including children). Of course, I was more interested in the platforms and what was happening there than staying in the waiting room.

The platforms at these busy stations were fascinating. There were always crowds at the times we travelled on a summer Friday evening. There were hundreds of people going on holidays overloaded with cases and bags, sweethearts saying tearful good-byes or delighted hellos, latecomers running to get their train at the last minute. Porters would be helping with luggage or driving electric tractors along the platforms pulling two or three trailers piled with mailbags and parcels and horns blowing to clear people out of the way. Everywhere there was the noise of whistles being blown, trains arriving and departing, loudspeaker announcements that no-one could understand and hustle and bustle and all the more exciting for that.

Snow Hill Station, Birmingham
Ben Brooksbank

But even the excitement could not dull a young boy or girl's appetite for sweet things. The fact that you could put a penny (or was it two?) into a slot machine, pull out a small drawer and get a thin bar of Cadbury's Milk or Fry's chocolate was not far short of miraculous. Another interesting object which seemed to be present at every main line station was the weighing machine. This was a huge machine with a large dial on which a red needle pointed to the correct weight when some one stood on the base and put their penny in the slot. Much amusement could be got by watching the various travellers step on the base and seeing their reactions to the weight shown and the complicated manoeuvres that allowed two people to get weighed separately while paying only *one* penny.

Even though the platforms provided many interesting things to see, nothing compared to what you saw once you had shown your ticket at the barrier and got to where your train was waiting. The huge locomotive was even bigger in reality than it seemed because only the top two thirds of the engine was visible above the platform level. The noise of the engine and sight of the steam were thrilling and frightening at the same time. A train coming in at the next platform in clouds of steam and the brakes squealing would make normal speech impossible. The smell of the smoke added to the sense of excitement. Then, it was time to get into the carriage – third class, of course. With the same unique English logic that called private schools "Public Schools", there were only two classes, first and third. Second class had disappeared long before, into the mists of the Victorian age and it seemed that no one had ever caught on to this fact.

Climbing up the steps into the carriage was no easy task when you were pulling a heavy case nearly as big as yourself. This was especially so when you were late and trying to get on to the train just as it started off. The excitement of running along the platform, pulling open the carriage door and falling up the steps was tempered by the fear that your mother would be left behind on the platform and that you would be on your own and on your way to Stafford or Crewe without her. (My father rarely accompanied us on this journey from Birmingham, as his two weeks' holiday only started in August and he followed us then).

Somehow, we always managed to get onto the train before it started or, at the latest, before the slowly moving train had picked up speed. This would not be possible now with diesel or electric power but the steam engines were always slow to pull away with their long tail of carriages. Also, the doors did not close automatically as nowadays, so there were always people yanking open the doors just as the train started to move and half climbing, half falling onto the train.

Usually, however, you were on the train in plenty of time and could lean out of the window at the door and watch the guard checking that everything was ready to go, looking at his pocket watch, raising his green flag and blowing his whistle. In this case, you also had the pleasure of seeing other people make a last-second dash for the train and, best of all, because children are not naturally sympathetic to strangers, sometimes see them fail to make it.

Although there were still some non-corridor trains which were made up of individual eight-seater compartments, each with its own door and no internal connection to the rest of the train (and some of them survived into the 1970s), most express train carriages had corridors along one side, leading to the compartments which were intended to seat up to eight people. The trick was to get into one of the compartments, close the sliding door with its glass panel and, whenever anyone else made to come in, look as if you were going to be noisy and awkward. This sometimes kept other people out and gave room to lie down on the (always dusty) bench seats. But often the trains were so full that not just the compartments but even the corridors were crowded with people sitting on cases or army or navy kitbags. For some reason, there always seemed to be a lot of National Servicemen, particularly sailors, travelling on our train.

Smoke gets in your eyes!
Ben Brooksbank

One of the pleasures of train travel in the 1950s for a young boy or girl was the fact that you could stand by the door and open the window. This was done by lifting the thick leather strap off the brass pin that held it in place and letting the window down as far as you wanted before clipping the pin onto another hole. The problem was the weight of the window, which made lowering it easy but closing it again another story entirely. Once the window was open, you could put your head right up to the gap and feel the air rushing past. As the train went round a bend, you could get smoke and even cinders blown into your eyes. This was not pleasant.

Most times, before you enjoyed the excitement for long, a grown-up would come along, close the window and spoil the fun, telling you not to lean out of the window unless you wanted your head knocked off by another train passing in the opposite direction. Or, if you were on a mail train, as we usually were, knocked off by the sack of mail that was hanging from a scaffold-like affair by the edge of the platform, waiting to be automatically collected by a scoop net extending from the mail van as your train thundered through a station without stopping.

Even the sounds made by trains were different to those made today. There was a lot more clanking of carriages. Unless you were in the first carriage after the locomotive, there was not so much engine noise as there is today in diesel trains which have the engines under the carriages because all the power was provided by the steam locomotive at the front of the train. But when you were moving fast, there was the constant *diddle-ee-dee, diddle-ee-dee* as the wheels crossed the short expansion gap between each length of rail (the rails were not welded in long sections, as nowadays) and the deeper *diddy-dee-dum* sound as they crossed over the points onto another track. But, wherever you were on the train, there was always the swaying of the carriage (much more than nowadays) and the piercing noise of the engine's whistle.

As we were taking the boat from Heysham in Lancashire to Belfast, we had to change trains at Crewe and board the express from London to Scotland. In those days it seemed almost impossible not to change trains in Crewe, no matter where you were going. This meant a dash from platform six to platform twelve, or something like that, with only a few minutes to make the change. Inevitably the connection was made and, even if the train from Birmingham had plenty of empty seats, the train from London that we were now boarding was always crowded.

From Crewe, the train thundered northwards into the gathering darkness, stopping only at Preston and Lancaster. Here, we would wait for maybe half an hour while the back carriages, where we sat, were decoupled from the main part of the train and another locomotive steamed to what had been the back of the train and pulled us into Heysham, which was the port for Belfast.

Getting off the train and on to the narrow gangplank to board the ship was always a high point in the journey, not least because the gangplank seemed to be just that – a plank about two and a half feet wide with a rail to hold onto and the sides covered by canvas. This gangplank was always very steep and bounced alarmingly with the weight of the crowd of people moving up it at the same time. But, at last, with a slightly relieved final step you were off the gangplank and on the ship, a real sea-going steamship. In the tradition of Columbus and of Storm Nelson of the Silver Fleet in the Eagle comic, the first job of any self-respecting eight to ten year old sailor, after carefully placing your case on the deck where your mother and other adults could trip over it, was to inspect the bows of the ship and check that that you were pointing in the right direction, even if the crew always managed to get this wrong.

If the train was crowded, it was only in the halfpenny (pronounced *"haypenny"*) place compared to the ship. We always sailed to Belfast at the end of July, on a Friday night and, so it seemed, did everybody else. Summer sailings at the weekend were classified as "controlled sailings" which meant you had to have not just a normal travel ticket but a sailing ticket, as well. The idea was to limit the number of people on the ship but it always seemed a very flexible limit when you were on board, having to step over people lying on the floor of the saloon deck or even on the steps leading down to it.

There was always a long wait for passengers from the last boat train to arrive but, eventually, everyone was on board. Now was the time to go up on deck and watch the gangplank being lowered to the dockside, feel the vibration of the engines deep below you and watch with interest the deckhands casting off the heavy ropes which were the last links between ship and shore.

Slowly, the ship, *your* ship, began to move, backwards at first or "slow astern" – the correct term, as you knew from reading the adventures of Storm Nelson and his Silver Fleet in the *Eagle*. Then, it would go about and head to the entrance to the harbour and, finally you were on the open sea, the *"High Seas"* and, if you were not quite heading for the *"Spanish Main"*, you were doing the next best thing and heading West or, at least, Northwest.

Until 1956, the ships sailing on the Heysham to Belfast route were the three RMS (Royal Mail Ship) steamers, the Dukes of Lancaster, Argyll and Rothesay, all built in 1928. We usually travelled on the *Duke of Lancaster* which had a particularly eventful career, catching fire and sinking in 1931 and then, after being salvaged, running aground twice and colliding on three occasions with other ships, sinking one of them, a coaster, in 1940. Nevertheless it and the others continued to serve the travellers to Belfast until 1956.

The ships were not nearly as comfortable as present-day ships and were not fitted with modern stabilisers, so they rolled and tossed in heavy seas in ways that passengers today rarely have to endure. The result was that, in rough weather, if you managed to keep your stomach under control, by the time you reached Belfast Lough, you felt as if you had made an epic voyage – even though it had only lasted seven or eight hours. And you had made this voyage on a ship that was a *real* ship and looked like one, not a floating shopping mall like today's massive cruise liners.

We would sail through the entrance to Belfast Lough early in the morning. On the right hand side, or *starboard* – the correct term, as every young mariner knew - was the rugged coast of County Antrim and the squat menace of Carrickfergus Castle, more than 750 years old. On the left, or port, side lay the gently rolling hills of County Down, where you could see the smoke of the early train taking workers to Harland & Wolff's enormous shipyard in Belfast.

Another hour on the ship and then we were tied up at the quayside and ready to disembark down a gangplank just as bouncy and scary as the one we had climbed up in Heysham the night before.

My grandad (my father's father) was there to meet us and help carry our luggage to his 1930s Hillman Minx saloon for the 17-mile journey from the quayside to his house in the small village of Drumaness. This normally took about forty minutes, or longer if I had to ask for a stop because I was feeling sick. The reason for this was partly I was of an age when many people got carsick and partly because of the engine fumes that managed to leak into the car. Apart from that, I thought the car had a certain character, being painted green and black and having running boards like the cars in the gangster films set in the 1930s. Many's the time I stood on these running boards, holding on to the car with my left arm hooked around a door pillar and the right hand holding my trusty tommy gun, as I sprayed bullets at the Black Hand Gang who were trying to muscle in on my territory. I have to regretfully confess that the car was always standing still by my Granddad's workshop and not screeching round a Chicago corner when these flights of fancy happened.

My grandad's Hillman Minx
Kay Keane

Drumaness

My grandad lived with my grandmother and the youngest three of their five children in a cottage attached to his garage and workshop just outside the small village of Drumaness, in the middle of County Down. One of my aunts and my uncle were only a few years older than I was. So for this reason I spent as much time as I could at this house.

It was there that I learned to ride my first two-wheel bike – one that my grandad had built the frame for – when I was five. The teaching system was simple. My older aunt would keep me steady by holding on to the saddle but when I got up a decent speed, she'd let go without telling me and I carried on by myself - for a while!

My granny could have been the model for an advertising agency's dream granny. She was small and plump, with bright red cheeks, glasses and a cheery disposition. She usually had flour on her apron because she baked every day. I particularly liked her flat soda griddle bread (a speciality in County Down and the adjoining counties) baked over a solid fuel range on a big round cast iron griddle. With fresh country butter and syrup spread on the bread while it was still hot, it became a feast.

The house had no running water or pump and the water was pulled up in a bucket on a rope from a shallow well. Incidentally, my granny paid a visit to us in Birmingham about 1955 and the thing which impressed her most was what she described as "the beautiful water" which we had in our house. Birmingham was one of the first cities in England to have a modern water supply, in this case, from the Elan Valley reservoirs in central Wales and its water was superior to that of most other places – certainly London.

As my Uncle Gerry was only five years older than I was, I used to pester him to play with me, which he would invariably do with good humour. Two of our favourite games (mine, anyway) were *Cowboys and Indians* and *Robin Hood*. As my grandparent's house was beside a small river and much of their two or three acres of land was low-lying and covered with rushes or small trees, we had an excellent play area for these games. Both of these games involved bows and arrows, which we made from the branches of the trees near the river. The bow would be about two and a half feet long and the arrows about one and a half, with the end padded and wrapped round with sacking. This padding did not prevent me getting a very sore black eye when my uncle seemed to think we were at the Battle of Hastings instead of the Little Big Horn and I ended up in the role of King Harold getting hit in the eye!

Another favourite game was our own version of *shove ha'penny (half penny)*. This was played more like a football match than normal shove ha'penny and consisted of a smooth wooden surface and a ha'penny for the ball and two teams of two large old pennies each. The idea was to give one of the pennies a sharp strike with a comb, ruler or even a third penny and to hit the ha'penny into the opposing goal which was defended by one of your opponent's pennies. Of course this gave ample opportunity for claiming fouls but it did develop hand-eye co-ordination skill in working out the angle of shots since the kernel of the game was a sort of simplified poor man's (or boy's) snooker without the cues and the only real soccer aspect was the goal at each end of the board.

By 1952, the Korean War was in its third year and my uncle had developed an interest in building scale models of the fighter aircraft used in the war. I would watch with interest, gradually turning into boredom as he took what seemed to be hours to carefully cut out spars from sheets of balsa wood and glued them together to form a fuselage frame. Then he would cover the frame with tissue paper, dampen it to shrink the paper tightly on to the frame and then paint the lot with dope to harden the tissue. Finally, he would fit a small *Jetex* rocket motor inside the fuselage and his North American *F-86 Sabre* or Russian *MiG-15* combat plane (he made both neutrally) was ready to fly.

My own model aircraft preference was for *Frog* aircraft which came in a kit with pre-shaped cardboard fuselage and fin, balsa wood wings and tailplanes, plastic propeller unit powered by a twisted rubber band and wire and plastic undercarriage. These slotted together and your flying model was ready in minutes rather than the hours needed to build one of my uncle's planes. These planes could fly for quite a while if you wound the propeller two hundred times or more before launching your *Spitfire, Hurricane or Mustang* into the skies. My uncle's planes and my simpler models were both usually hand launched but the *Frog* models could actually take off from the ground. We built an improvised secret runway under the trees near the river and soon we were the most daring of air aces. Many years later, I made a model aeroplane for one of my sons out of a cornflakes box and fitted it with a propeller and undercarriage which I had found in a drawer. I was pleasantly surprised when it actually flew very well.

My other uncle, who was a few years younger than my father, was in the Merchant Navy and brought back presents from many of the places he visited. One of these was a monkey called "Brazzy" (because he came from Brazil) which delighted us children by climbing up onto the clothes drying rack which hung from the ceiling of the kitchen and throwing down nuts and other things at anyone who had annoyed or scared him. Unfortunately, Brazzy could not adapt to the Irish climate and died after only a few months. This same uncle once gave my mother an alligator skin handbag. The leather was a beautiful golden-brown colour but my mother put it away at the bottom of a drawer and never used it because the flap of the bag was made out of the head and front paws of a small alligator and the eyes were replaced with big glass marbles. She thought it was the ugliest thing imaginable. It was actually very impressive but perhaps slightly scary.

Since my grandad had the only petrol pump for miles around, there were always plenty of visitors. The pump was hand operated, which meant that, as a handle was pumped from side to side, the petrol filled a glass container holding half a gallon. When the container was full, a lever was pulled to release the half-gallon into the car's fuel tank and the operation was repeated until the required amount of petrol was delivered. It was a slow process but allowed plenty of time to chat to the customers. One of the most popular customers, as far as I was concerned, was Geordie Brennan. Geordie had the only ice cream van for miles around and his arrival was always the signal to rush into my granny and ask if I could have an ice cream.

Geordie had a big metal tub of ice cream in the back of his van and he sold two types of ice cream from it – *"Pokes"* and *"Sliders"*. *Pokes* were cones, filled from the tub with a scoop shaped like a big spoon. The high point of getting one of these was when he poured a stream of strawberry sauce over the vanilla ball in the cone. *Sliders* were wafers and Geordie created these by digging a sort of topless rectangular box into the tub of ice cream. When he had filled the box, he would slide a metal plate across the top of the ice cream, cutting off the excess and leaving a rectangle of delicious ice cream which was then ready for a wafer to be placed on the top and another on the bottom. And then he would hand over his creation to an eager hand in exchange for two pence.

Geordie's ice creams became world famous - at least in Drumaness and surrounding areas - and are still strong in my memory over sixty years on.

Some days, when my uncle had specific work to do, or it was raining, I had to find my own amusement. Often this would involve going into my grandad's garage workshop and watching him working on his lathe. On the wall he had a Castrol oil chart showing what lubrication was recommended for various cars. Even in the 1950s, some of the names of these cars were echoes of a different age. On the list were such names as AC, Alvis, Armstrong Sidderley, Auto Union (now Audi), Buick, Chevrolet, Chrysler, Citroën, Daimler, Frazer-Nash, Hillman, Humber, Lagonda, Lanchester, Lea-Francis, Mercedes, Simca, Singer, Sunbeam-Talbot, and many more long-gone models but not, oddly, Bentley or Rolls Royce.

As my grandad's garage was on the main road between Belfast and Newcastle we often saw army convoys travelling to Belfast from the army camp at Ballykinlar, near Newcastle. Mostly these convoys comprised these were troop-carrying lorries but sometimes there were more exotic vehicles like half-track armoured vehicles.

Unlike in Great Britain, the police were always armed. The Royal Ulster Constabulary (RUC) grew out of the old Royal Irish Constabulary when most of Ireland gained independence as the Irish Free State in 1922. The RIC had been basically a *gendarmerie* to enforce British rule in Ireland and the RUC inherited many of its attitudes, particularly the fear that "Ulster" and its Protestant people were under constant threat from the rest of Catholic Ireland. Generally however, the regular police in County Down got on tolerably, or even reasonably, well with the Catholic community but it could be very different with the Special Constabulary.

The "B" Specials were volunteers recruited from the locality and were 100% Protestant (the regular RUC had about one-sixth of its number who were Catholic) and they regarded themselves as a militia determined to defend a "Protestant Parliament for a Protestant People" against Catholic "traitors". This was at a time when elections to the semi-independent Parliament at Stormont, just outside Belfast were regularly gerrymandered to give the "right" results without any interference from successive British Governments which simply ignored any irregularities and refused for nearly fifty years to answer any questions in the Westminster Parliament about what was going on in "Ulster".

While I was used to seeing policemen carrying a revolver as part of their normal equipment, I remember being surprised in the mid-fifties to see a "B" Special guarding a sandbagged border police barracks, armed with a Thompson sub-machine gun (a "Tommy gun", as shown in gangster films). The police in both parts of Ireland always served in "barracks", never police "stations" and older people still refer to the local "barracks" to this day.

From 1956 until about 1960, the IRA or Irish Republican Army (which claimed authority for its actions from the armed struggle between 1919 and 1921 for an Ireland free from Britain but which refused to accept the Irish Government in Dublin as legitimate because it had effectively accepted the partition of Ireland) carried out a relatively low level campaign of violence against border police barracks and it was during this campaign that I saw the "B" Special mentioned above. Shortly after the end of that campaign, an incident happened which illustrated the more normal level of mutual, though slightly wary, tolerance between the regular RUC and the Catholic community in many rural areas like mid County Down.

I was about eighteen at the time and out with my father and an uncle at a country pub. At that time the law laid down that pubs closed at 10pm and about twenty minutes after that time, the bar was still full. The door opened and a RUC constable walked in and looked round at the now quiet drinkers.

"Will ye ever ["so and so"] get out of here now. It's well after closing time and we're going to raid the place in ten minutes!" and he turned on his heel and walked out.

Everyone ordered another drink (or two) and stood outside the pub drinking it as the police car, or "squad car" as it was called in those days, pulled up, four policemen got out and went into the pub where they stayed long enough to have a drink, then came out and said goodnight to the people outside, addressing many by name in a friendly manner and drove off.

Of course, everyone went back into the pub for a few more drinks!

The Loop

But, back to my earlier days. My other grandparents lived on a small farm which, because it was largely surrounded by a large bend in a river, was called the *"Loop"*. It was just two miles away from my grandad's garage. My grandfather had a damaged leg due to an accident and so the farm of 49 acres was run by my uncle and one farm labourer. Until about 1957, when I was 14, my uncle did not have a tractor and all the ploughing and pulling power was provided by two enormous grey shire horses; Blossom and Fanny. I can remember my uncle walking behind them as he ploughed a furrow, as straight as a ruler, across the hilly field, or sitting on the seat of the reaping machine pulled by one of these horses as he harvested the fields of oats or barley. These small fields were one reason why working horses remained on so many farms until well into the 1950s.

The landscape was made up mainly of *"drumlins"* separated by poorly drained low-lying meadows. Drumlins were small hills left haphazardly on top of the ground rock by rapidly melting glaciers at the end of the last Ice Age, about 10,000 years ago. The effect on the landscape was described as "basket of eggs". If you can imagine an old-fashioned wicker basket (as in fairy tale pictures) containing loose eggs, it gives you an idea of the up and down nature of the small hills, jumbled together. It also explains why drainage was so difficult in the lower lying areas between the hills. The soil was a jumble of fertile soil mixed up with stones and even boulders carried by the glaciers and dumped just wherever the ice melted. There was no grading of soil as in other areas where the Ice Age took a longer period of time to come to an end.

Intensive farming in 1950 - (helping my Uncle James to feed the hens)

The steepness of these little hills made tractor ploughing difficult in the small fields of the time. Few fields were bigger than five acres and many were much smaller. Another reason for using horses was that they were cheaper than tractors and, in that part of County Down, this was an important factor because few of the farmers had much spare cash or, even, much cash at all. Most farmers grew their own potatoes, turnips, cabbage and carrots and got their eggs from their own hens (the money got from selling eggs over their own needs was probably the only money many farmers' wives had on a weekly basis). It was one of my jobs every morning to go hunting for eggs laid along the hedges and field banks by hens which refused the comfort of the henhouses for their laying.

Another of my jobs, this one in cooperation with my cousins about the same age as me, was to follow the *reaper* during harvest. The reaper needed two men to operate it, one to guide the horse and a second one to handle a sort of big wooden rake which pressed a swathe of corn down on to the cutting bar of the machine.

Reaper in operation
Michael Rice

The reaper cut the stalks of the oats and left them lying on the ground to be gathered up by hand and tied into sheaves and then leaning five sheaves together to form a *"stook"*. My younger cousins and I would follow behind, picking up the loose stalks and binding them by hand using some of the stalks themselves. There was a skill in tying the stalks so that the sheaf held together properly and it was a skill which I was only moderately good at. The work was very sore on a city-living boy's back. The other problems I had were:

(a) being brought up in the city, I wasn't nearly as efficient or quick at this work as my cousins; and

(b) in those days, beautiful looking grain fields concealed a lot of thistles which scratched and stung young arms in spite of thick grey flannel shirt sleeves buttoned down to the wrists.

Gathering up the corn and binding it
Michael Rice

Another job which I had to help with was stacking the hay into *hayricks* to dry in the fields. These ricks were about four or five feet high and looked like smallish haystacks. They were then covered at the top with thick sacks or a couple of sheaves carefully spread out to keep the rain off the rest of the hay. When the hay was dried sufficiently, the ricks would be demolished and put on to a horse-drawn cart for transport to the *"haggard"* or hay yard where they were built up into a huge hay*stack*, ten or more feet high and roughly the same in diameter. Both hayricks and stack were built up by workers using pitchforks but, while this was easy enough for the ricks, building a haystack meant one or more men standing on top of the ever growing hill of hay and catching the clumps thrown up by the pitchforks of the other workers on the ground.

All this was dusty and very thirsty work and when my grandmother blew her whistle to summon the children to the farm-house to collect billycans of strong tea and pieces of bread thickly spread with her home made country butter, there was a welcome sigh of relief and a few minutes rest for the workers.

Preparing to start threshing
Michael Rice

I was only occasionally at the Loop when the corn threshing took place, unless it was a particularly good summer and the corn was harvested early, before I had to go back to Birmingham and school. Threshing was the process by which the grain was separated from the stalks and it was a very labour intensive job. The local farmers gathered at each farm to help one another in turn. The threshing machine, often owned by a contractor, would arrive at a particular farm, towed by a tractor or a traction engine which also provided the power to operate the machine. The corn was brought in a cart and loaded into a hopper on top of the thresher. The power was connected by a belt from the flywheel of the traction engine or tractor power take-off and the operation began.

For us youngsters, the sight and sounds of the threshing machine as it shook and creaked was very impressive. By some magical method, once the straw was fed into the hopper by the team of men standing on top of the thresher, the rapidly moving bars and sieves inside the machine beat the ears of corn so that they were separated from the straw, the straw was ejected at the back of the thresher to be collected by another team of men for future use as fodder for the farm animals and the grain fell out of a chute at the front into bags, ready to be sent to the local mill to be turned into oatmeal. For the men at work, with all the chaff and bits of straw flying about, this was even thirstier work than the reaping. It could also cause serious illness if the dust got into the lungs over a long period of time.

The straw, now minus the grain
Michael Rice

The final stage of threshing, bagging the grain
Michael Rice

As the Loop was a small farm of only 49 acres and only part of it was used for growing grain, the threshing took up only part of the day. When the work was done, all the men would retire to the kitchen for their dinner which would be boiled potatoes in their skins piled in a big dish in the centre of the table, boiled bacon and cabbage, plenty of butter for the potatoes, washed down with milk or buttermilk. This meal would be a very social affair, indeed one of the main ways of strengthening the social network among the local farmers who needed to cooperate on many occasions to work their farms. Afterwards, the thresher would be moved to the next farm where the process would start again.

My uncle kept no more than two or three milking cows at any one time. These were brought into the stone-built milking byre (a milking *parlour* was something fancy and only seen in the pictures in the *Farmers' Weekly)* and tied up. This byre had once been whitewashed but there was little sign of that left. The hygiene preparation was that my uncle washed his hands in cold water tipped out from a bucket and then briefly hand washed the cows' teats and udders with water from the same bucket. Then, a quick squeeze to send a small stream of milk onto the floor to ensure the teat was not blocked and the milking began.

The milk for the farmhouse was directed into a clean enamelled bucket held between my uncle's knees, or sometimes at one of the semi-wild cats that would come too close as they waited impatiently for their share of the warm milk. Once the enamelled bucket was filled, the milk for the calves would fill another one or two ordinary buckets, with a little poured out for the cats.

There was no heating in the byre and no slatted floor where the waste from the cows was automatically washed away, only a drainage channel which would be cleared by shovel and then washed down with water flung down from a spare bucket. In fact the waste treatment was no more advanced for the farmhouse. The toilet was a dry privy, about thirty yards away from the house on the edge of the farmyard. The toilet seat was just a wide plank fixed along the back wall and boxed in at the front. The hole cut in the plank was just above the edge of the farmyard dung heap. The *Farmers' Weekly* provided both reading matter and toilet paper. But the two most interesting things about this very basic toilet were that there was never an unpleasant smell and there were never any flies in it, no matter how warm the weather.

The milk for our use was taken to the farmhouse and stored in the milk room. This was a small room on the north side of the house and was, therefore, the coolest place in the house. There was no refrigerator, as there was no electricity. The window was always open during hot weather, with wire mesh keeping out the flies. The milk for drinking was fresh every day and, if there was too much, it would be converted into butter. Because the milk was exactly as it came from the cow, without any treatment, and was kept in a clean enamel bowl in the milk room, the cream soon floated to the top of the milk and was skimmed off. The cream was then placed in a hand operated barrel churn which was spun over and over around a horizontal axis.

After a while, the butter would form clots and soon there would be enough butter to take out of the churn. Any buttermilk in the churn would be poured out and kept for my grandparents to drink and for baking and the butter squeezed between two wooden paddles to get rid of excess moisture. With salt added, this country butter was so much better than the butter you bought from a shop, especially if it was spread on freshly baked and still warm bread.

The bread both my grandmothers made was soda bread, baked into a flat cake, divided into four *"farls"* on a flat cast iron *griddle* about fifteen inches in diameter. At the Loop, this was placed on top of the big *American range* which stood out about four feet from the wall in the kitchen and which was kept lit from morning to bedtime, as it was the only source of heat in the house, apart from rarely used fireplaces in the parlour – the best room which was only used in exceptional cases or during *wakes* or funeral times – and the bedrooms. One of my jobs each evening was to collect enough sticks from around the hedges for the range and to fetch coal in a bucket from the storeroom in the farmyard.

The kitchen was the main room in the house and was where all the cooking was done, as well as where all meals were taken and where everyone gathered, family, neighbours and the extra harvest helpers alike. Off the kitchen was a small scullery with a stone sink and water supplied from the pump outside the door. There were no water taps, so the water had to be pumped by hand into a bucket and carried into the scullery. All clothes washing was done here and the clothes hung out to dry on the line or, in the case of big items like sheets, on the hedges near the house.

As well as my grandmother's soda bread, we also had the bread van come twice a week from the Ormeau Bakery in Belfast. The bread van would drive up the two hundred yard long lane (or *lonan*, in the local dialect) to the farmhouse. Before it reached the bend half way, I would have rushed from wherever I was to meet it because it delivered not only bread but Paris buns, iced buns, fruit squares and other such delights. These were laid out in big, shallow trays, which the bread man pulled out like drawers for my grandmother's and my inspection. My grandmother spoiled me and I was always pleased with her purchases.

I have already mentioned that there was no electricity. Light was provided by a paraffin-burning *Tilley lamp* which hung from the wooden ceiling in the kitchen. This needed some skill to get going. Paraffin oil was poured into the tank in the base of the lamp where it was pressurised by working the built-in hand pump. This action forced the paraffin up the narrow column to a small piece of felt-like material clipped onto the lamp just below the mantle. This material had been soaked in methylated spirits which was lit to light the cotton mesh mantle which acted much as a filament in an incandescent electric bulb. The result was a very bright but harsh light which needed reinforcing from time to time by further use of the hand pump attached to the paraffin tank.

By the way, methylated spirits had a distinctive "medical" smell and was used in a variety of ways in the home, for example in cleaning windows, removing ink stains and as an aid to reducing bruises.

Tales From The Loop

My grandfather was in his seventies in the 1950s and had an injured leg, so he no longer had much to do with the active running of the farm, this being my Uncle James's job. But he had an inexhaustible fund of stories, mostly about the fairies and how local people had upset them and lived to regret it. I could never work out if my grandfather really believed in the fairies, or not. I suppose that uncertainty was the sign of a good storyteller.

It is important to understand that the fairies in Irish folklore are very different from those commonly found in fairytales as popularised in books and Disney films. They don't have wings and, even more importantly, Irish fairies, if not some of the stories about them, are based on historical fact.

In Ireland the fairies are a distorted memory of the Bronze Age people who inhabited the island before the Celts arrived about 2,600 years ago. They were smaller and darker than the Celts and their bronze weapons and tools were no match for the iron swords, spears and ploughs of the Celts. Gradually, the pre-Celtic people were forced into the areas of poorer soils and into the hills, forests and wilder places. They would avoid the Celtic farmsteads but might rustle cattle or sheep from them.

They would also avoid as much as possible anywhere there was evidence of iron weapons. The Celtic farmers would leave something of small value made of iron in full view, perhaps hanging on a wall, believing this would scare off the pre-Celtic people. Over time, this iron object usually came to be an old horseshoe which was too worn to be useful. Eventually the iron horseshoe was thought to bring good luck to the homestead where it was displayed, as the original reason for its display was forgotten. Indeed the idea of good luck was transferred from the iron of the horseshoe to the horseshoe shape itself, hence the belief that the points of the horseshoe should point up, so that the luck does not drain away. Even today, brides may carry a cardboard horseshoe and wedding cards often have horseshoes printed on them but we have totally forgotten that the "good luck" is due to the iron of the horseshoe and not its shape.

Many "fairy" stories can be found all over Ireland with very little variation but, whichever part of the country you are in, the stories are almost always localised and linked to a real person who lived in that locality. My grandfather used to tell a story about a local man called Casemy *(pronounced "Caze-me")*. Now, Casemy lived about half a mile from my grandfather's house and the remains of his cottage could still be seen until very recently. He was, by all accounts, a cantankerous and unhelpful character, perhaps because of the very noticeable hump he had on his back.

Coming back home from the market one rainy evening in November, Casemy was driving along in his horse-drawn cart when someone called him.

"Casemy! Are you going home?"

"I am, not that it is any of your business," said Casemy to a small man standing by the side of the road.

"I'm soaked," said the man *"And I have a blister on my foot. Would you give me a lift? It wouldn't take you much out of your way."*

"I would not", said Casemy and he drove on.

Two weeks later Johnny, a neighbour of Casemy, who coincidently also had a hump on his back, was driving in his cart along the same stretch of road. The weather was still bad. A small man was standing in the rain at the side of the road. He called out.

"Johnny! Are you going home?"

"I am."

"Would you give me a lift? It wouldn't take you much out of your way."

"I would, surely. Jump up on the cart here."

Now, my grandfather never actually said there was any connection between these two evenings and what happened next but everyone in the countryside knew that, from the day the Johnny gave the small man the lift, Casemy's hump grew bigger and bigger, while Johnny's hump grew smaller and smaller, until it disappeared entirely.

Another story, told by my Uncle Charlie, my mother's sister's husband, related how he went into one of his fields one day. This field was at the top of a hill and contained what was locally known as a fairy fort. The "fort" consisted of a mound surrounded by a circular ditch and may originally have been an enclosure where cattle could be kept for safety if there was feuding or rustling in the neighbourhood. Anyway, on this day, my uncle went into the field as he had done many times before to count his cattle. The only difference on this occasion was that, when he had finished counting the cattle, he could not find his way out of the field. Even though he walked the entire length of the hedge, he could not find the gate – it had simply vanished! It was not until he had completely circled the field seven times (seven being a magical number) that he was able to find the gate and leave the fairy fort field.

Like my grandfather, my uncle told the story as it happened to him with an intensity and detail that was entirely convincing. Like the previous story about Casemy's hump, this story about being trapped in a field well known to the storyteller can be found in many of the counties of Ireland.

In the field in front of my grandfather's farmhouse there was a small rocky outcrop that was a nuisance because it prevented the plough getting to a sizeable area in the corner of the field. On the outcrop grew a single thorn tree. Like other similar lone thorn trees growing in the middle of a field, it was called the *"Fairy Thorn"*.

Stories used to be told about strange and beautiful soft music coming from the branches of the tree at nighttime. My grandfather and his son, my uncle James, were advised on many occasions to grub up the tree and blast out the rock to clear the way for the plough but neither of them would ever do it.

"It's done me no harm and I'll do it no harm."

I don't know what my grandfather and Uncle Charlie thought but my Uncle James would never admit to belief in the fairies. But the fact is that the fairy thorn is still there, untouched, in that field which is now owned by one of my cousins.

Fairy thorns also remain untouched in fields in many country places in Ireland and there have been instances, even in recent years, when local workmen have refused to cut them down when they are in the path of a proposed new road. Either workmen have had to be brought from Dublin or some other city to do the job, or the line of the road has been altered to bypass the tree. But *nobody* will admit to believing in the fairies.

Casemy had a part to play in another incident which, I know actually happened because I knew one of the people involved, although a long time after the incident. Casemy eventually died and was laid out on his bed for the *"wake"*, when people would come by and pay their respects to the bereaved family, kneel by the bedside and say a prayer asking God for mercy on Casemy's soul and then go and have a cup of tea or a drop of whiskey, according to taste, in the kitchen. Because of the large hump on his back, Casemy had to be tied down to the bed with rope, so that he would lie flat. During the course of the evening all the neighbours would visit the house.

About ten o'clock, when it was nearly dark, Billy arrived to pay his respects. Now, Billy liked a drink and he liked a *few* drinks even better. He had already called at more than one pub before arriving at the wake. Anyway, Billy went into the bedroom and knelt down to say a prayer. Everyone else was in the kitchen, talking, drinking tea or whiskey and eating the sandwiches and cake that were customarily served.

Everyone, that is, except one of my mother's cousins, Hugh-Willie Flynn and one of his friends. These two, both about seventeen years old, crept in to the bedroom and found Billy still kneeling down but dozing. The two lads crept under the bed, made enough noise to half wake Billy up and then cut the rope. Casemy's body, propelled by his hump, slowly sat up in the bed - to the horrified gaze of Billy who, with a shriek, jumped up and leapt through the closed window, not to be seen again until very late the next day when he was sure Casemy was safely in his grave.

Hugh-Willie was well known as a lady's man and was often seeing two or even three girls at the same time. Sometimes this double or triple life got too complicated, even for him and he found that he had arranged to see two girls at the same time. When this happened, he called on his brother, Stephen, for help. Although Stephen was a few years older than Hugh-Willie, the two brothers were remarkably alike in both looks and manner and Stephen would meet Hugh-Willie's "extra" girl that evening. This happened on several occasions and it is claimed in the family that none of the girls ever realised that they had been romanced by a "substitute" Hugh-Willie.

As my two sets of grandparents lived only about two miles apart I would divide my time between the two homes. By the time I was about nine, I was allowed to ride a bike between the two places – in the morning from my mother's home farm to spend the day with my uncle at the garage and back in the evening before it got dark. Of course, when you are nine, there are always interesting things which keep your attention and make you late leaving to go back to your grandfather's farm. So, often the light was beginning to fade before I mounted an old bike for the return journey to my grandparent's farm along the quiet country roads.

Half way between the two houses was a stretch of about a hundred yards where the road was overshadowed by tall trees whose branches curved over and formed a shadowy tunnel. By day the tunnel gave welcome shade when the weather was hot. But by the time I reached there, it would be dark under these trees, bats would be flying about and the tunnel became a menacing place. To make matters worse, Hugh Phillips lived in a dark and run down house just at this spot.

Hugh was a bit odd and, to a young boy, scary. He would stand by the door of his house and watch everyone who went by. He never spoke, always wore black and he had a long, wild-looking beard. Hugh was, in fact, harmless but he looked "different" and I was one of many children who were more than a little scared of him and I dreaded going past his house as it was getting dark. I would slow down as the bike got near his house, conserving all my energy until I was nearly at the start of the overhanging trees, then pedal like mad through the dark tunnel, past Hugh's house until I had got through to the other side and into the clearer twilight of open countryside. Only then would I slow down and start breathing again. This terror happened every time I went past his house in the evening but I never mentioned it to my mother when I reached my grandfather's farm safely. A boy in those days just did not admit to being scared.

On a more pleasant note, although the road between my two sets of grandparents was only about two miles long, it always took me much longer than necessary to walk this distance on a sunny day because I could not pass a blackberry bush without sampling the fruit. On one occasion I had just left my grandparents' house and was walking along the main Belfast to Newcastle road (which in those days was not all that busy), sampling the blackberries growing alongside as I went when it started to rain. There were no trees to shelter under but, and this is the interesting fact, I did not get wet! I was happily picking blackberries in the sunshine on one side of the road which was about five or six yards wide, while the rain was falling heavily on the tarmac only ten feet away from me.

One of the pleasant things about picking blackberries and eating them at the same time was that no two berries tasted the same. One would be soft and sweet and the next would be somewhat harder and not quite as ripe, so it would have a slightly tarter taste and the contrast made the sweet berries taste even better. This variety of taste could also be found when I was "helping" my mother in the kitchen by shelling peas. This job demanded that the peas be sampled as they came out of the pod. Some would be sweet, others would be harder with a slightly nutty flavour but I would enjoy them all. My job as a pea-sheller would come to an abrupt end when my mother noticed that most of the pile of pea pods were empty but there were very few peas in the saucepan. Most people nowadays do not experience this pleasure of the variety of tastes because frozen peas have the same taste from the first ones that come out of the packet in the freezer to the last.

I inherited this love of peas in the pod from my father who was virtually banned by my mother from going near the kitchen when she was preparing peas. I remember one occasion when he took me to see one of his uncles who lived in a cottage in Drumaness with a quarter-acre garden in front. As we went through the garden gate, my father saw the peas growing. We diverted from the path to the front door to the pea plants and it took us over twenty minutes getting from the gate to the door. I never found out my great-uncle's opinion about our attack on his pea plantation.

Back In Birmingham

Back in Birmingham and other cities, the streets and the general environment were much quieter than nowadays. There was much less motor traffic and many more bicycles. You would hear the call of the rag and bone man, driving his horse and cart and looking for anything householders wanted to throw out. Keen gardeners were always pleased to see the rag and bone man or, more accurately, his horse because there was the chance of collecting fresh and still warm droppings which were highly prized as fertiliser for roses and other flowers. It was not unusual to see the wives of more than one gardener (the men would be at work) rushing out into the street with a hand shovel to scoop up the precious manure.

There were no portable radios, or ghetto blasters but you would hear many men and delivery boys whistling the latest tunes or old favourites. *Ronnie Ronalde* even became one of the most popular performers in Britain in the 1950s with his ability to whistle bird songs and popular tunes. Yet, how often do you hear anyone whistling now? I sometimes still whistle as I walk along the street but I can't remember when I last heard someone else do so.

At every busy corner in the city centre in the late afternoon, you would hear the cry of: *"Spatcher my-el, spatcher my-el"*, which was a local abbreviation of: *"Excuse me sir, would you care to buy a copy of the Evening Dispatch or Birmingham Mail?"*

All the newspapers of the time used to publish several editions each day, with the front page often radically different for each edition. This was a remarkable feat when you consider that there was no computer typesetting. Each time a page was changed, the new paragraphs had to be assembled letter by letter by a sort of complicated typewriter from a frame which contained hundreds of cast lead letters and the typesetters or compositors were members of a highly skilled trade.

Many people lived within walking distance of their place of work. Most of those who had to travel further did so on the bus, on bicycles or on motorbikes. The buses were similar to the old London Routemasters, with the driver sitting in a small self-contained compartment and a conductor responsible for collecting fares and keeping order. The most memorable thing about these buses was the open platform at the back.

One of the essential skills for a boy or young man (and, sometimes, not so young men) to master was the ability to chase a bus after it had left the stop and to grab hold of the pole at the back and then leap on to the platform. Another, equally essential skill was to drop off the platform while the bus was still travelling without ending up sprawled in the road. This latter manoeuvre could only be achieved if you leaned back out of the platform, let go of the pole and stepped backwards at the correct angle. Of course, neither jumping on nor jumping off the bus were things that could be mastered by girls. Or was it maybe that girls were too sensible to show off in this manner like boys did?

Almost all the buses in cities were double-deckers and smoking was allowed on the upper deck only. The conductor or conductress took the fares and issued the tickets which, on a few services were still cardboard tickets held in place by spring clips on a wooden clip board (hence the nickname *"clippies"* for conductresses). There were no season tickets and getting onto the bus was a very quick affair because no one held up the queue by fumbling for their tickets or change as can happen today.

Birmingham bus showing rear platform and pole to help jumping on and off while the bus was moving

outercirclebus.com

Someone enjoying her work

outercirclebus.com

Bus conductors and conductresses sometimes took delight in waiting until someone running for the bus had almost reached the stop and ringing the bell so the driver started off, leaving the not-quite passenger disappointed and puffing at the bus stop. Obviously the conductress in the above picture would not do such a dirty trick!

Bus timetables were posted at every stage bus stop and could more or less be relied on, although complaints about waiting ages for a bus then two or three arriving at once were common. If the driver was ahead of schedule, there was a built-in corrective (in Birmingham, at least) in that along each route there were clocks where the driver had to check in.

When the driver was early, he had to wait until the correct time until he clocked in. One of these clocking-in points on the Inner Circle route, which I took to secondary school, was at a bridge over the Birmingham to Wolverhampton canal. During the late 1950s, as the bus waited there for five or more minutes to get back on schedule, you could look down on some of the last working commercial barges chugging slowly along the canal, carrying cement, coal or road building materials.

These were all that remained of the hundreds of barges which had once moved thousands of tons of freight along Birmingham's canals every day. On one occasion, I even saw what must surely have been the last horse-drawn barge in the Midlands as I waited for the bus to continue on its way. The Birmingham Canal Navigation system covered a total of almost 160 miles at its peak. Now it is down to about 100 miles serving leisure traffic almost exclusively – something unthought of as I looked down from the top deck of the number 8 Inner Circle bus.

Most of the country bus services between towns were operated by single-deckers. Many of these buses had a ladder for the conductor to climb up on to the roof and load boxes, suitcases or even crates containing chickens or racing pigeons onto the roof rack.

There were still a few tram routes in Birmingham up to 1953. One of them ran from close to my primary school past the municipal swimming baths in Aston. Every week, we would be taken there on the tram for our swimming session. The tram had a major attraction – wooden floors. Obviously, these were thoughtfully designed so that small boys could run upstairs, get to the front (wooden) bench above the driver's position and bang their feet on the floor until the driver sent the conductor up to put a stop to it – by which time the front bench would be mysteriously empty and every boy would be sitting quietly, well away from the front and looking innocently out of the window.

The trams had an open driving platform at each end and were noisy and draughty as they rattled and swayed along. They were powered by electricity from overhead wires, collected by trolley poles which sometimes lost contact with those wires. When that happened, the tram slowed to a halt and the pole had to be manually reconnected to the wire by the conductor with the aid of a rope attached to the pole. This sight always attracted attention from any small boys and girls who were around.

Carl's Tram Line Story

Cycling to and from school in 1950s Birmingham provided many challenges. Quite apart from the dangers posed by what I considered were multitudes of motor vehicles, all seemingly intent on using the same small space occupied by my bicycle, there were the dreaded tram tracks.

In those days there were still a few tram routes left in Birmingham and a large portion of my route to school followed one of these routes. Now for the most part the tram tracks ran merrily along in a central reservation between roadways. However, when reaching various built-up or shopping areas the tram tracks ran down the middle of the road. For those unfamiliar with trams I should explain that unlike railway lines, tram tracks were laid flush with the road surface and had a deep groove in the centre – just about the same width as a bicycle tyre.

At around 5 pm one weekday the inevitable happened. I was cycling through Northfield – a busy shopping area. Traffic was heavy at this time of day, but I was only minutes away from home. At this point I had to make a right turn across the traffic flow and the tram tracks to get home. Seeing a break in traffic I started across the road. All did not go as planned. The road surface was still wet from an earlier shower and when I was about to cross the tram tracks diagonally, my tyres slid down into the tracks. Try as I might I could not get out.

At this moment in time a number 72 tram appeared behind me. When I say appeared, I mean that a rather large double-decker behemoth was hurtling down the same tracks towards me – with no obvious sign of stopping. Feeling somewhat alarmed (to say the least), I frantically tried to out pedal it.

Suddenly, to my horror, I came to a rather abrupt stop. Glancing down I saw that the raincoat which I had tied to my handlebars had come loose and was now jamming the bike's front wheel. The tram still came on. In desperation I leapt off my bike, picked it up and made a dash for it.

The tram rattled and swayed past.

I said extra bedtime prayers that night.

Birmingham also had five trolley bus routes. Starting in 1922 and lasting until 1951, the trolley buses offered a more comfortable ride than the trams and could cope with steep hills more easily than the buses of the time. They were quieter than either the trams or buses. Also, they offered more flexibility than the trams because they could manoeuvre like ordinary buses but, like trams, they were limited in range by the overhead electric lines which were necessary. In other parts of Britain, trolley buses continued in use up to the mid to late sixties and even into the seventies in Cardiff, Walsall, Teeside, and Bradford where the last working run of the last public trolley bus service in Britain took place on 26th March 1972.

Early 1950s Ford Popular
Michael Rice

Although there far fewer cars than today, the numbers were increasing all the time as more people began to travel to work in their car. These would mostly be people like doctors and other professionals but, as Birmingham was the centre of the motor industry, cars were owned by more working class people than in most other cities. Almost all the cars on the road were British. The main exception from 1953 was the Volkswagen Beetle, which brought a new standard of reliability because of its quality of build and its air-cooled engine at the rear of the car. Among the most common cars of the 1950s were Morris Minors and Oxfords (which continued in production in India as the Hindustan Ambassador until May, 2014), Austin A30s and A40s, Ford Anglias, Populars and Prefects and the more modern looking Consuls, Zephyrs and Zodiacs.

But, starting in 1959, with the introduction of the Mini and followed soon by Ford's Capri, Cortina and Corsair, car ownership in Britain soared. Sporty types could even buy a Jaguar E-type from 1961 – if they could afford the price of £2,098 which was more than four times the 1959 cost of the basic Mini's £497!

Morris Minor with split windscreen
outercirclebus.com

Apart from the Beetle, nearly all cars were supplied with a starting handle as water-cooled engines could be difficult to start because self starters were liable to be affected by cold or damp weather. The starting handle was inserted into the crankshaft through a hole at the bottom of the radiator grill and then turned clockwise. Usually it took two or three attempts before the engine would start. The most memorable thing about the starting handle was that, if it kicked back during the cranking process, the person holding the handle could end up with a very sore thumb or even a broken one. Learning how to hold a starting handle properly, with the thumb on the same side of the handle as the fingers, was something you got to know very quickly.

As well as being used to start the engine, a starting handle could get a car out of a difficult situation if it was stuck in mud and could go neither forward or backward. If you put the car into reverse gear then turned the starting handle, the car would jerk backwards. Doing this several times could get the car out or the mud and onto the hard surface again. The process was, however, slow and tiring for the person turning the handle, not to mention being potentially dangerous to the thumb.

One of the significant differences between cars of the fifties and today's models was the necessity of the *choke*. This controlled the richness of the petrol/air mixture supplied to the engine. By pulling out the choke lever on the dashboard, the driver could increase the percentage of petrol in the mixture and so make it easier to start the engine on cold mornings. However, too much choke would mean the engine would flood and not start at all. Again, the choke had to be pushed back as soon as the engine was firing properly or the petrol consumption would be too great. It was alleged that some lady drivers who complained about the heavy petrol consumption of their cars were causing the problem by leaving the choke pulled out and hanging their handbag on it. But this allegation may have just been part of many comedians' act.

Another difference between cars of my young days and today was that indicator lights were uncommon, except in the most recent models. Most cars up to the early fifties indicated that they were turning right or left by using *trafficators*. These were yellow or orange plastic semaphore arms about nine inches long which would stick out from the door pillars to show the direction of turning. Although most of these had a small light inside, they were much less easy to see than the flashing indicators that were beginning to come into widespread use. In fact many drivers still indicated which way they were turning by using hand signals.

Just as almost all the cars on the road were British, so were nearly all the motorbikes, which many people rode to work. Ariels, BSAs, Matchless, Nortons, Royal Enfields and Triumphs were the most common but German NSUs could also be seen. Like Morris Oxford cars until recently, some Royal Enfield models are still made in India. Becoming widespread in the fifties and early sixties were motor scooters, mostly Italian like Vespsa and Lambrettas. Their popularity was due to their relative affordability and their modern streamlined design. The fashion conscious "Mods" took to them with enthusiasm, following the success of the 1953 Gregory Peck/Audrey Hepburn film, *Roman Holiday*. The motor bikes, on the other hand, were the preferred form of transport for the "Rockers" who were the up to date descendents of the "Teddy Boys" of the early fifties. Groups of Mods and Rockers frequently clashed with each other, culminating in riots in Brighton in 1964.

One of the favourite (but rare) road sights was provided by the road repair gangs. The noise of the pneumatic drills breaking up the tarmac, the navvies with their picks and shovels and the smell of the freshly heated tar, ready to be spread on the repaired surface were all highlights of a boy's observations of the world around. But the most exciting things of all were the sight and sounds of the

91

steamroller slowly trundling along with its enormous iron roller and wheels and its huge flywheel spinning rapidly and apparently dangerously close to the driver standing on the rear platform.

The *navvies*, by the way, were so called because they were the successors of the *"navigators"* who built the original *"navigations"*, that is, canals, of the late eighteenth and early nineteenth centuries.

An exciting sight
Bill Nicholls

A fairly frequent sight on main roads was the AA man, in his khaki uniform, or the RAC man in his more officer-like grey/blue. These could often be seen parked beside an AA or RAC telephone box, waiting for calls for assistance from members of the Automobile Association or the more "upper class" Royal Auto-mobile Club. Their uniforms were quite military, the RAC men in particular looking like cavalry officers in their jodhpurs and riding gaiters and their military style caps. They rode motorbikes with sidecars in which were all the tools necessary to deal with most types of car breakdown and minor mishaps. They were required to salute members who displayed the respective badge on their car, unless it was unsafe to do so.

Even more common were the police telephone boxes that were dotted around main streets in cities and towns. These contained a telephone with a direct link to the local police station had a roof-top blue light which would flash to alert a policeman on the beat to call the station for instructions. The telephones could also be used by members of the public to alert the police about an accident or crime taking place. This was, of course, before mobile phones and at a time when few people had a phone in their house.

If you lived in a city or large town, you could expect to see a police constable patrolling his beat every day and, although he didn't have today's rapid response or communications systems to back him up, the very fact that people were aware that a policeman who knew the local area and its inhabitants was patrolling somewhere nearby gave a sense of security and helped to keep crime levels down. That, and the fact that many a boy doing something he shouldn't be doing got a clip across the ear from a hefty policeman, meant that justice and punishment were swift and not dragged for weeks or months through the courts in the case of some minor offence.

Uniforms were much in evidence in the streets, with more policemen, postmen, bus drivers and conductors to be seen than today. But the one person in uniform that ordinary people did not want to see was a boy or young man on a red bicycle or motorbike – the telegram boy. The telegram boy usually carried something unwanted in the leather pouch on his belt – a message of death or accident concerning a loved one (always a worry, especially when troops were involved in fighting overseas) or a summons to the bedside of a dying relative. Unless it was the day of a wedding when people who could not attend the ceremony might wire their best wishes, the arrival of a telegram was rarely good news. Among the few times a telegram was welcomed was if it gave instructions to start a new job immediately because private telephones were few and far between or even one from the King or Queen, congratulating someone on reaching their hundredth birthday. Companies might welcome a telegram giving news of orders for urgent supplies, but most people preferred to do without telegrams, thank you very much.

If people needed to make a phone call, most of them would make it from one of the red cast iron and glass public phone boxes which could be found in cities every few hundred yards. Even in many country areas on main roads, phone boxes were fairly common. To make a call, you put two large penny coins into the money slot by the receiver and dialled the number you required. When you heard the person answer, followed by the sound of rapid pips, you pressed the button marked "A" to allow the coins to fall into the money box and you could then speak to whoever you were calling. If the number was engaged, you pressed button "B" and got your money back.

Your two pennies allowed a local call for three minutes, as far as I can remember, after which the pips started again and you had a short time to get another two pence into the slot before the call was automatically ended. Because of the brief interval when you could hear the person at the other end and before the pips started, you could be sure who was answering the call. This meant that, if you were old enough to have a "posh" girlfriend - that is one whose family had a phone in their house - and were calling her but her mother (who didn't approve of you) answered, you could put the receiver down, press button "B", get your two pence back and save them until later when you hoped it would be your girlfriend who would answer this time.

Another useful thing about these telephones was that sometimes callers who had not made a successful connection forgot to press button "B" and the two pence stayed in the box until a young boy or girl pressed that button and the forgotten money came out and provided the capital needed for a Fry's chocolate bar or *twenty* blackjack liquorice sweets.

If you wanted to make a long distance call, that is to the next town or further afield, you first had to call the operator who would make the connection for you, tell you how much to put in the slot for a three minute call and interrupt after that time to ask if you wanted to continue the call by putting in more money. International calls (way beyond my personal experience) had to be booked in advance through the operator and were *very*, *very* expensive.

If you were among the few people who had a telephone at home, you almost certainly had a "party" line. This was a line shared between two or maybe more houses. If someone else on the shared line picked up their receiver while you were already on a call, they could hear your conversation and *vice versa*. However, as people did not make all that many calls, this overhearing happened only occasionally but it had to be kept in mind if you were discussing romantic or other private matters.

Sport

The main sports were football from autumn to spring and cricket in summer. Rugby was only a mass working class interest, as Rugby *League*, in the North of England and so it rarely featured in the national press or on the radio. Rugby *Union*, which was reported in the national papers and on the radio (but not to anything the same extent as today) was mostly confined to people from Public School backgrounds and in the professions, particularly the medical profession.

There were (and are) two main football clubs in Birmingham – Aston Villa *(the Villa)* and Birmingham City *(the Blues)* and a third - West Bromwich Albion - just outside the city boundary. The latter was known as *the Baggies* because the players wore old-fashioned long shorts after most other teams had adopted a more modern style. All three clubs usually played in the First Division (at that time, the highest division). The lower divisions were the Second Division and the Third Division, North and Third Division, South.

Most teams were still recognisably local teams, with a substantial number of players from the local area, although transfers for the best players were becoming common, with the first £50,000 fee being paid in 1957 to Leeds United by the Italian club Juventus for John Charles. Many players, however, remained with one or two clubs throughout their career, notably Tom Finney, who stayed with Preston North End from 1946 to 1960 and Billy Wright who joined Wolverhampton Wanderers as a 14 year old in 1939 and stayed with them until 1959 when he moved into management. Both men, along with hundreds of others had their playing careers shortened by the Second World War when the League competitions were suspended.

Players did not have the luxury lifestyles of today, they lived among the fans and, until 1961, the best paid earned a maximum of only £20 a week – a good wage, worth about £390 in 2014, and the same as a good toolmaker in one of Birmingham's bigger factories. Pat Saward, Aston Villa captain in 1959 lived a short distance away from my house in Villa Street which is described in the early pages of this book. But he lived in *digs,* not even in a flat and certainly not like players do today. Most players at the time who were away from home would be living in similar accommodation.

According to the Professional Footballers' Association, a Manchester United and England player could have earned about £32 a week including all bonuses during the 1956-57 season. In January 1961 the wages cap was removed and Johnny Haynes of Fulham became the first player to earn £100 per week which was worth about £1,900 in 2014 values or about one-ninth of the *average* weekly pay of today's Premier League players and less than half of the *average* pay of Championship players. Of course, most top footballers in 1961 were still paid less than Johnny Haynes's £100 per week.

Cricket was unrivalled as the great pastime from May to the end of August. Test cricket, county cricket, village, works and parish teams would take over Lord's, the Oval, Old Trafford, Headingley, Edgbaston, Trent Bridge and countless club, village, college, school and local parks cricket grounds. Indeed, in some ways, cricket was more universal than football as some schools played rugby rather than soccer but virtually *all* boys' schools played cricket.

The great names of the fifties were the ones that inspired my interest in cricket. The explosive fast bowlers, especially Yorkshire and England bowler Fred Trueman and Australia's Ray Lindwall were my greatest heroes and the ones on which I modelled my own bowling - in my imagination, if not reality. But how could anyone forget Dennis Compton (who played both cricket and football for England), Len Hutton, Godfrey Evans, and Jim Laker, who took nineteen Australian wickets in the fourth Test at Old Trafford in 1956, Tony Lock, Peter May or the "terrible twins" of Surrey, Alec and Eric Bedser? Peter Loader and Johnny Wardle are among many, not so well remembered now, who also performed wonders at test and county level.

Keith Miller, the Australian all-rounder who was Lindwall's frequent bowling partner, was always a problem for English batsmen and bowlers alike. The West Indies side of 1950 won their first victory in England with the "three Ws", Worrell, Weekes and Walcott and two young spin bowlers, Sonny Ramadhin and Alf Valentine who had played only two first class matches each before the start of the tour but who devastated the English batting in the second Test at Lord's and who were rewarded by a well known calypso song being written about them. These are only a few of the cricketers who shone in the seemingly never-ending sunshine of the 1950s.

At the other end of the scale from Test and County teams were hundreds of local village, parish and works teams which played each match as if they were Tests. The team my father played for was unusual in that it was based around a Catholic parish, although not every team member was Catholic. As it had no home ground, every match, except some played on a local park's pitch, was an away match. This often meant a welcome Sunday afternoon trip to the country. I still remember watching my father, our team's wicketkeeper and Vice-captain, taking up his position very close behind the wicket even when our fast bowler, Wally McMahon, was in full spate. On one occasion this close stance led to him being knocked out when being unsighted by the batsman. Other, more pleasant, memories for a twelve year old were the lemonade, sandwiches and cake between innings, the company of the Captain's twelve year old daughter and our innocent games while the match went on.

One other sport which I particularly liked watching was the speedway racing at the Perry Barr track in north Birmingham about a mile and a half from where I lived in the fifties. I would go with my father on a Friday or Saturday night and the crowds, noise and smell of hot oil and roaring exhausts were all thrilling for a young boy. The way the riders skidded their powerful bikes round the bends, with one foot gouging trenches in the cinder track, throwing up showers of small cinders up into the hair of spectators beside the barriers and lodging in their clothes must have been the despair of many wives and mothers faced with washing those same clothes. For a young boy, this was not something he thought about. Just being with your father for a few hours, experiencing the noise and excitement was enough. That, and the pleasurable sensation of scratching at the cinders caught in your hair!

If the way the speedway riders steadied themselves with one foot as they went round the bends was impressive, even more so was the cornering technique of the TT riders as they raced their Nortons, AJSs, NSUs, Augustas and Moto Guzzis in the many road races of the time. As they leaned over to take the corners, with their knee only a couple of inches above the tarmac, what kept them from losing balance and falling over? Surely the only possible explanation was *magic*. There was no other logical reason. That, anyway, was what went through my mind as I watched the Ulster Grand Prix riders roar past on the Dundrod circuit near Belfast with my grandfather. Geoff Duke and John Surtees were the most famous of these riders in the 1950s.

Other sports which have since become very popular, such as tennis and golf, did not register in our determinedly working class world of the 1950s and hockey was beyond the pale altogether since, in the eyes of any right thinking boy, only *girls* played hockey.

World Affairs

I remember being outside in our back yard one day in the early 1950s and hearing the sound of aircraft in the sky. This was a rare occurrence as we lived on the opposite side of Birmingham to the airport. A flight of six or so American B-36 "Peacemaker" bombers were flying overhead. These were enormous for the time, or even today, fifty-four yards long and a wingspan of nearly eighty yards. The most obviously impressive thing about the planes, apart from the size, was that they were powered by six huge propeller engines *and* four jet engines, giving a range of over 6,000 miles. The planes were probably on their way from America to one of the US Air Force bases in East Anglia.

Of the 384 B-36s built, none saw any active combat duty but they were used for high altitude reconnaissance during the Korean War. This war was the first international event that I was aware of and, even then only slightly. In fact, the only event that I can even vaguely recall is the three day stand by the Gloucestershire Regiment (the Glorious Glosters) at the *Imjin River* in 1951 although outnumbered by seven to one and I only remember that because it was the lead story on BBC *Radio Newsreel* which my parents listened to at seven o'clock in the evening.

It was a different story three years later at the *Battle of Dien Bien Phu* in Vietnam (then French Indo China). By then, I was almost 11 years old and more aware of what was happening in the outside world because I was a keen reader of the *Daily Mirror*. This battle was the decisive event in the long running war in Indo-China. French paratroops, Foreign Legion troops and pro-French Vietnamese soldiers were surrounded and outnumbered four to one by communist Vietminh forces. The battle, in which the French were in an ultimately impossible position, lasted fifty-four days and was noteworthy for many heroic sorties by the heavily outnumbered French, for paratroop reinforcements dropping into the besieged base in the most difficult, indeed hopeless, situations and for one woman, Geneviève de Gallard.

She was one of a number of nurses on the French air force flights evacuating the wounded. She was stranded in Dien Bien Phu on March 28th when her plane was destroyed by the Vietminh and she remained there until the garrison fell six weeks later. She was the only female nurse there and was dubbed *"the Angel of Dien Bien Phu"* by both French and British newspapers. Her bravery and devotion to duty were reported at length in our daily paper, the *Daily Mirror,* then an excellent <u>news</u>paper, not the largely celebrity- and gossip-driven publication it became much later. She was awarded the highest French honours, the *Légion d'Honneur* and the *Croix de Guerre* and was made an honorary member of the Foreign Legion, all of which while the siege was going on. She also received the highest American civilian award, the *Presidential Medal of Freedom* during a visit to the United States after her release from captivity.

Two and a half years later, when I was thirteen, in October 1956, another international event happened which had an even stronger effect on me. This was the Hungarian uprising against the communist Government when thousands of people took to the streets and effectively overthrew the communist system, giving the hope of a democratic future. The secret police soon started firing on the crowds and the Russian Red Army, which had many garrisons in Hungary, intervened with its allies to put down the uprising.

Vicious street fighting went on for several days, and Red Army tanks were attacked with *Molotov cocktails* - bottles filled with petrol with a rag stuffed into the top and then lit. The insurgents would creep up behind a tank, open the badly protected fuel tank cap at the rear of the tank and drop the blazing Molotov cocktail into the fuel tank – with predictable results. What made a lasting impression on me was that some of the Hungarian patriots attack- ing the Russian tanks in this way were *boys and girls of my age or only slightly older.*

I remember listening to the news from Hungary on the BBC Home Service each evening describing the unequal struggle between the Hungarians and the Red Army and its Eastern European allies and especially the last broadcast of the English language service as the Soviet troops were about to storm the building containing the makeshift studio. After making a final impassioned appeal for help from the Western countries, the station closed with:

"This is Radio Free Hungary, signing off".

Britain and France were, however, more concerned at the time with events in Egypt. In July of 1956 a previous offer from the United States to help finance the building of the Aswan Dam across the River Nile for much needed irrigation and electricity generation was withdrawn because Egypt was forging closer ties with the Soviet Union. In retaliation, the Egyptian leader, Colonel Nasser, nationalised the Suez Canal which had been largely owned and operated for over eighty years by an international company dominated by Britain and France. The Canal was of great economic and symbolic importance to both these countries who decided to encourage a war between Egypt and Israel. Then Britain and France would intervene and send troops to separate the warring armies and "protect the Canal from damage" and also by the way, help the Israelis to seize control of the Sinai Peninsula. They were confident of backing from the United States but this backing did not materialise. President Eisenhower forced Britain and France into a humiliating withdrawal that left Egypt in control of the Canal. This failed adventure showed just how much power had seeped away from Britain in the eleven years since the victory over Germany in 1945.

But not all the news in the fifties was about wars. In 1951 the Festival of Britain was held. This was not as successful as was hoped because it was seen by many as too political and aimed at celebrating the achievements in the arts and civic developments of the post-war Labour Governments. More enthusiastically embraced in the following year was the idea of the New Elizabethan Age which began with the accession of Princess Elizabeth to the throne in February, 1952. This was hailed by the Conservative Prime Minister, Winston Churchill, and taken up by the newspapers. Perhaps, it was just an excuse to forget about the austerity of the years since the end of the Second World War. The shortages, rationing and bombed sites which still remained were associated by many with Labour by people who forgot about the many social advances achieved since 1945 like improvements in education, housing and, above all, the National Health Service which was, at the time of its introduction, in 1948, probably the most advanced health service in the world as far as ease of access for ordinary people.

This idea of a new age, reviving the spirit of adventure and exploration of the 16th century, grew as the year and a half to the new Queen's Coronation went on. Britain introduced the first jet passenger airliner – the De Haviland Comet in 1952 and the plane was enthusiastically welcomed by Government and passengers as an example of Britain's place at the leading edge of aviation. A few early accidents were initially put down to pilot error but in 1954 two fatal crashes over the Mediterranean Sea led to all Comets being grounded while intensive investigations were undertaken. These showed that there were major faults in the design leading to catastrophic metal fatigue. By the time Comet flights resumed in 1958 with a new improved Comet IV version, larger, faster and longer range planes like the Boeing 707 were beginning to establish an American dominance in the air which lasted almost un-challenged for two decades until Airbus came on the scene in the early 1970s.

However, on Coronation Day, the Comet's problems were largely in the future and Britain could convince itself that it had regained much of its former influence among the world as the leader of the British Commonwealth.

The Royal Navy was still the second, or perhaps third largest navy in the world and its vessels patrolled all the oceans and major seas, protecting international shipping and showing the flag to remind the world that Britain was still a force to be reckoned with.

The Royal Air Force was starting to be supplied with new aircraft like the *English Electric Canberra* and others were being test flown or in development, such as the *Hawker Hunter* fighter, the radically new delta-winged *Gloster Javelin* and, especially, the three V-bombers, *Vickers Valiant*, *Avro Vulcan* and *Handley-Page Victor*, all three capable (or so we were told) of delivering a devastating nuclear blow against the Soviet Union if it should be so reckless to attack Britain or its allies.

The Army was licking its wounds after the vicious but eventually stalemated Korean War but still had bases in every continent. Britain may have lost India (partitioned into India and Pakistan), Burma and Ceylon (Sri Lanka) but all except Burma remained in the British Commonwealth, Moreover, Britain still ruled much of Africa, the West Indies and many islands in the Pacific Ocean. All in all, when Queen Elizabeth II was crowned in Westminster Abbey on 2nd June 1953, she reigned over a country which, with its imperial remnants, could still claim to be the third most powerful in the world, after the United States and the Soviet Union. (This was three years before the humiliation of Suez, mentioned above.)

The Coronation

The morning of the Coronation on June 2nd 1953 dawned with rain and cold winds but the country's spirits were raised by the news which reached London during the morning that the British Everest expedition, led by Colonel John Hunt, had succeeded in reaching the summit of Mount Everest. The climbers who actually reached the top first were a New Zealander, Edmund Hillary and a Nepalese Sherpa, Tenzing Norgay. As the news of this British triumph was being broadcast on BBC radio and television on the morning of the Coronation, it was regarded as a good omen for the *"New Elizabethan Age"*. An interesting contrast to today is that the summit of Everest was actually reached on May 29th but it took four days for the news to reach London.

I don't remember much about the Coronation itself. The ceremony was not something that a nearly ten-year-old boy was particularly interested in. It was broadcast on television but neither we nor any of our neighbours had a television. I probably saw a British Movietone newsreel some days later at the cinema or "picture house", as we called it. I do remember getting a Coronation mug, like everyone else at my primary school while my younger brother, only three years old, got a crown shaped moneybox. I considered that he got the better deal.

What I do remember about that day is the street party we had where everyone in the neighbourhood turned out and where we children enjoyed more cake, jelly and condensed milk and other treats than most of us had seen before. After that came games and races down the street and the day turned out to be enjoyable in spite of the unseasonable weather. My brother won a prize for running while I got a prize (I forget what) for reciting a humorous poem about a postman.

To the best of my knowledge, nobody near us in our street had television at the time of the Coronation. Apart from the newspapers and local gossip, all the news was provided by radio, commonly known at the time as the *"wireless"* because the programmes were transmitted directly through the air and not through wires like telegraph messages, and by the newsreels at the local picture house, as the cinema was then called by most people.

The Wireless

The wireless was not only a source of news; it was the main provider of culture and entertainment. The BBC was the only broadcaster and it had two main radio channels – the *Home Service*, which provided news, discussion, some light classical music (most classical music and serious drama were on the high-brow on the *Third Programme*), drama and some comedy and the *Light Programme*, which provided popular and light music, quiz programmes, most comedy and adventure drama.

The most popular music programmes included *Desert Island Discs*, with its dreamy signature tune, *"Sleepy Lagoon"*, *Housewives' Choice, Children's Choice* (with Uncle Mac) on Saturdays – *"The Laughing Policeman"* and *"The Teddy Bears' Picnic"* were very popular requests, *Worker's' Playtime, Two Way Family Favourites*, which linked families in Britain with husbands and sons serving in the armed forces stationed in Germany and various Commonwealth postings (the signature tune was *"With a Song in my Heart"*).

Among my own favourite programmes were: *Dick Barton - Special Agent* (a daily fifteen minute segment tragically replaced by *The Archers* in 1951) with its evocative signature tune, *"The Devil's Galop" (sic)*. (By the way, the Archers started as a dramatised information programme sponsored by the Ministry of Agriculture aimed at educating farmers about new farming developments and techniques and it only became popular after it changed into "an everyday story of country folk"). Other favourites were *Paul Temple* – a detective series, introduced by its theme music - *"The Coronation Scot"*, the Western series *Riders of the Range* with *"Ghost Riders in the Sky"* as its signature tune, *Our Day and Age* – a true life series about people faced with hard decisions or situations out of the ordinary, *Twenty Questions*, comedies like *Take it from Here, Hancock's Half Hour, Round the Horne, The Goon Show, Educating Archie* (in which the hero was a ventriloquist's dummy), and, above all, the science fiction adventure of *Journey into Space*, one of the most popular programmes of the 1950s.

In one episode of *Journey into Space*, Lemmy the radio operator, asks a friendly alien to let him see what he really looks like. The alien refuses, saying that Lemmy would not be able to stand the sight but Lemmy insists. Reluctantly, the alien reveals what he really looks like and the scream of terror from Lemmy, with which the episode ends, gave a better picture of horror in the listener's head than any image shown on television or the cinema screen.

Children's Hour, from five o'clock to six, was one of the highlights of the day. Aimed at children from five to fifteen, it tried to be both educational and entertaining and, by and large, succeeded in both. It featured series taken from well-known books, like Kipling's *Just So Stories, Sherlock Holmes, Winnie the Pooh, Worzel Gummidge* and the *Jennings* school stories and many more.

Our wireless sets of the time were noteworthy for the number of radio stations featured on the tuning dial. Many, if not most, of these were continental stations that could not be received unless you lived in the southeast of England, the major exception being *Radio Luxembourg*. Although I recognised many of the continental names like Paris, Rome and Berlin, some were unfamiliar like Allouis, Beromunster and Helsingfors.

Radio Luxembourg, which broadcast in English each evening from about 6 pm to midnight, was the source of programmes like *Dan Dare, Pilot of the Future* (a must-listen-to for an avid reader of the *Eagle* comic), *Take Your Pick* - a general knowledge game show with a series of 12 boxes containing prizes and box 13, which could contain either a valuable prize, such as a holiday or a washing machine, or a booby prize like a piece of old rope; included in the show was the *Yes/No interlude* when a contestant had to answer rapid-fire questions for one minute without using the words "yes" or "no" - It's not as easy as it sounds. Radio Luxembourg also outshone the BBC in its emphasis on the *Top Twenty* hit songs.

But the one thing for which the station became most famous in Britain and which *everybody* who listened to Radio Luxembourg in the late fifties and early sixties remembers was an advertisement. Horace Batchelor advertised his *Infra-Draw* method of betting on the football pools every week for many years and his West Country accent became recognisable to anyone who tuned into Radio Luxembourg as he gave his postal address as "Horace Batchelor, Keynsham, Bristol". Every week, he invited people to send him ten shillings (50p) to enter his Infra-Draw method and, for years, thousands of people did just that, in fact up to 5,000 entries a day were handled at the Keynsham office. He only took payment if the bets he placed for his subscribers won.

The football pools were the National Lottery of the day. In the *Treble Chance* selection, if you could pick out eight draws (later, eight score draws) out of the fifty or so games listed, you had a chance of winning, or sharing in, the enormous amount of £70,000 (worth over £1,200,000 in 2014) which was the top prize on offer each week.

We didn't have a television until I was nearly eighteen in 1961, when we moved house to a semi-detached three-bedroom house in Handsworth about a mile away from Villa Street but a world apart. Our new house, built in 1933, was a typical three bedroomed, semi-detached inter-war family home, with a front and back garden and a concrete garage built later by the side of the house. But the biggest change was the indoor bathroom and toilet. My father paid £2,100 for it with a mortgage obtained with the influence of his employer, since his age of forty-five was above that when banks would normally provide finance.

Before our move, the only television we saw on a regular basis was between seven o'clock and half nine on Sunday evenings after the evening Church service when we visited a friend of my mother's while my father and her husband went for a drink at the local parish club.

Every week, our programme was the same – first, a Western or crime series like *Gunsmoke, Maverick, Hawaiian Eye* or *77 Sunset Strip*, followed by *Sunday Night at the London Palladium* – a variety show during which *Take Your Pick* (transferred from Radio Luxembourg) was a highlight, a switch to the BBC at nine for the news and then home.

I enjoyed my television interval each week but I was brought up listening to the radio and, looking back I can understand the answer given by a schoolboy who was asked shortly after his parents had bought their first television set:

Which do you prefer, television or radio?"
"I think I prefer the radio."
"Oh, why?"
"Because the pictures are better."

I think that comment sums up very nicely the difference between the world of imagination in the 1950s, when each one of us created *our own* pictures inside our head from what we heard on the radio, and today's world where children are bombarded by a stream of images reflecting either a dumbed-down reality or *someone else's* vision of *their* imagination. On the other hand, radio could never compete with television in areas such as nature programmes, or where someone was demonstrating how something worked, to give just two examples.

The wireless was also the main source of popular songs. In the early to mid 1950s romantic ballads dominated the newly published Top Twenty. Songs by Bing Crosby, such as *"The Isle of Innisfree"*, from the John Wayne and Maureen O'Hara film *The Quiet Man*, *"Once I had a Secret Love"* by Doris Day, *"Three Coins in the Fountain"* by Frank Sinatra, *"Softly, Softly"* by the Belfast singer Ruby Murray (who set a record with five songs in the top twenty in the same week) were extremely popular, together with other American singers like Perry Como (*"Don't let the stars get in your eyes"*, *"Hot Diggity, Dog Ziggity, Boom what you do to me"* and many later hits), Guy Mitchell *("She wears red feathers and a huly, huly skirt"*, *"In a pawn shop on the the corner"*, *"My truly, truly fair"*), Jo

Stafford *("Shrimp boats is a-comin' "), "You belong to me" ["By the pyramids along the Nile"]*) and British ones like Vera Lynn, Alma Cogan and Jimmy Young. There were unusual hit songs too, like the winning song at the 1953 Llangollen (Wales) International Eisteddfod. Sung in German by the Obernkirchen Children's Choir *"The Happy Wanderer"* spent a total of 26 weeks in the British Hit parade and became a worldwide success.

But the top earning entertainer of the early fifties was an Irishman, Josef Locke, who sang such favourites as *"I'll take you home again, Kathleen", "Galway Bay", "Return to Sorrento", "Blaze Away", "Hear My Song, Violetta"*, and many popular songs from operettas, like the *"Drinking Song"* from the *Student Prince* and *"Goodbye"* from *The White Horse Inn.* Such was Josef Locke's success that the taxman wanted to take up to 19s 6d (97) in the pound tax from his earnings. Naturally, Josef did not think this rate of tax was justified and he went back to Ireland for some years, only returning to Britain after agreeing a tax settlement with Her Majesty's Customs and Revenue.

A different style of music that became popular in 1955 was Skiffle, an up-tempo style of playing with three main musical "instruments". These were:

1   a washboard, as used at the time by most housewives to scrub dirt out of clothes;

2   a large tea chest with a broom handle at one corner and string stretched from the top of the handle to the opposite corner of the tea chest and substituting for a double bass; and

3   a cheap Spanish (*not* electric) guitar or, sometimes, a banjo.

With these low cost or no cost instruments, a new type of music was invented. The most famous British skiffle player was Lonnie Donegan whose first hit was *"Rock Island Line"*, followed by *"Puttin' on the Agony, Puttin' on the Style"* and *"Does your Chewing Gum lose its Flavour on the Bedpost Overnight?"* Donegan's style of music inspired many famous stars, including Mick Jagger and the Beatles, the latter originating as a skiffle band called the Quarrymen.

From 1955, another new style of singer began to appear. It was in January when Bill Haley and His Comets burst into the Top twenty with *Rock Around the Clock* that the music scene changed forever. The Rock'n'Roll era had begun. Eddie Cochrane, Chuck Berry, Buddy Holly, Cliff Richard, Elvis, Manfred Mann, Freddie and the Dreamers, Gerry and the Pacemakers, Tommy Steele Lulu, Dusty Springfield and many, many more. But there was still room for the top American and British stars of the fifties, for ballad singers like Michael Holliday, Donald Peers, Nina and Frederick, for the melodic sound of the Supremes and other Motown groups, for Helen Shapiro and Susan Maugham, the Seekers and for jazz bands like Acker Bilk's and Kenny Ball's.

There was even room for Jimmy Shand's Scottish dance band to have a very popular television show *"The White Heather Club"* from 1958 to 1968 with accordians, kilts, ladies in tartan dresses and dances like the Dashing White Sergeant and the Gay Gordons ("gay" in its then usual meaning of "happy" or "jolly").

Comics, Books and The Pictures

My world of imagination (or *day dreaming* if truth were told) was also nourished by the comics and books I read. I was always fond of reading and, like most other children in the 1950s, I could hardly wait until it was time to get the *Radio Fun*, the *Dandy*, *Beano*, and later on the *Wizard* and, best of all, the *Eagle*.

The *Radio Fun* featured such comedy stars as Arthur Askey, Jimmy Edwards, Jimmy Jewel and Ben Warris and Norman Wisdom. The *Dandy* and its stablemate, the *Beano*, were eagerly awaited by millions of youngsters each week. We would laugh at the adventures of Korky the Kat, Desperate Dan's struggles to get peace long enough to eat his cow pie with the horns pushing through the pastry and the tail hanging over the edge of the dish and at Beryl the Peril causing chaos, all of these in the *Dandy*. In the *Beano*, Biffo the Bear, Lord Snooty and his Pals, Dennis the Menace, Roger the Dodger and Minnie the Minx gave hours of (nearly) innocent, anarchic fun. The *Wizard* was different. Although it had some picture stories strips, it was notable for its prose adventure and sporting stories. The most famous story was *"Wilson the Wonder Athlete"*. Wilson was well over a hundred years old but he had the strength and speed of someone in his prime due to a secret potion he had been given by an even older) hermit. As a result of his secret, Wilson was outstanding at any sport he took up, in particular cricket and athletics.

The *Rover* and *Hotspur* were also popular but, my favourite comic, by a long way, was the *Eagle*, which I awaited with impatience every Friday. It was originally conceived and edited by Marcus Morris, a Church of England minister who felt that there was a need for a children's magazine which entertained, and educated its readers and which had a high moral tone and promoted an idealised version of perceived "British" values. All the heroes were examples of courage, loyalty and were always true to their word, no matter what the difficulty.

Among the most famous strips were *"Dan Dare, Pilot of the Future"* (a future in which the International Space Fleet was led by

Britain and headquartered in England), the Western *"Riders of the Range"* and *"Storm Nelson"*, a sort of sea going righter of wrongs with his Silver Fleet of sailing ship, helicopter and mini-submarine. Other favourites were *"Luck of the Legion"*, *"PC49"* and an advertisement strip for Wall's Ice Cream featuring the crime-fighting adventures of *Tommy Walls*, who always came up trumps after he had made the *"W"* sign with his hands.

Biographies, of real people, such as Jesus, St. Paul, Marco Polo, St. Vincent de Paul, Lord Nelson, Abraham Lincoln, Winston Churchill, Field Marshal Montgomery of Alamein and his greatly admired enemy, Field Marshal Rommel of the German Afrika Korps, filled the back page. Cutaway drawings showed how various engineering system and developments worked. Examples included: railway locomotives, how mail bags were collected and sorted as the mail train thundered through a station without stopping, how the Navy's newest aircraft carrier *HMS Eagle* worked, how the tube system operated under London and an imagined international airport of the 1980s with atomic powered rocket planes and many, many more. Added to all this were the sports pages, competitions and other things of interest. What more could a boy want in a comic?

I think it is true to say that the *Eagle* of the 1950s set a standard for picture comics that was rarely equalled before or since. Companion comics connected with the *Eagle* were *Girl*, *Robin* and *Swift*, the latter two aimed at younger children.

In emergency, as when I was stuck in my grandparents' house in Ireland because of heavy rain and my uncle was not around to be pestered, I must confess to occasionally sneaking a look at my Aunt Eileen's *Girls' Crystal* or *School Friend*. But I would never admit to doing so. At my other grandparents' farmhouse, matters were even worse and emergency reading depended on the children's pages of my grandmother's *Peoples Friend* or *Red Letter* or, in desperation, *The Farmer's Weekly.*

Another source of reading excitement was provided by the American Comics like *Superman* and *Batman.* Not only did these bring in new adventure heroes but the inside covers carried small advertisements for such essential boyish needs as periscopes to spy round corners, secret codes, books to teach you how to throw your voice or perform magic tricks, and even X-ray glasses with the selling point that, with these glasses, you just happened to be able to see through girls' dresses! I never knew of anyone actually buying any of these offers, not even the X-ray glasses.

Just William?

When it was my birthday or Christmas, there would usually be at least one present of a book or books. I enjoyed books ranging from long established classics like *Treasure Island* or *Robinson Crusoe* to more modern series such as the *Just William* books about a ten year old always plotting adventures and getting into scrapes and the *Famous Five* series about four children and a dog always plotting adventures and getting into scrapes. Often the *Five* would unmask some spy or other villain and keep him in captivity until handing him over to the police, or help rescue people from danger. *William*, on the other hand, usually unmasked and imprisoned some totally blameless character and generally wreaked havoc – but (almost) always with the best of intentions.

The *Biggles* books by W. E. Johns about an intrepid ace pilot and his group of friends fired up the aerial ambitions of many schoolboys and countless Westerns were read under the bedclothes. The public library service was very good in Birmingham, both for giving a taste for adventure and for more practical books like "*1,001 Things for a Boy to Make*" (and "*1,001 Things for a Girl to Make*"). The former told you how to make such things as balsa wood or paper aeroplanes, a sailing boat, a submarine, a boat powered by camphor oil, a crystal set radio receiver, an intercom system using two cans and a long piece of string, a periscope, a heliograph, a tank using cotton reels, a rubber band and a match, a kite and 990 other useful and interesting things. Naturally, I had no personal knowledge of the second book.

But back to the adventure books. Anything suggesting pirates in places with exotic names or daring deeds in the Wild West drew me like a magnet. Port of Spain, Vera Cruz, San Juan, Santo Domingo, Zanzibar, Dead Men's Gulch, Apache Pass, Amarillo – these were all names that sparked my imagination and guaranteed that I would soon be reading about galleons sailing the Spanish Main, pieces of eight, buried treasure, or how to avoid being captured by Geronimo.

More adventures and laughs were to be had at the local picture house or cinema, in my case the *Villa Cross* picture house. This was a typical local cinema of the time, maybe somewhat bigger than usual, with 1,200 seats on two levels and moulded plaster decorative features on the walls and ceiling. There were two programme changes a week and each programme would consist of two feature films and a newsreel and, sometimes, a cartoon. My mother and I would go at least once a week and among the many films we saw at the time were *Shane, Calamity Jane, The Quiet Man, Seven Brides for Seven Brothers, The King and I, Treasure Island, Robin Hood and his Merrie Men, Peter Pan, The Lady and the Tramp, Around the World in 80 Days,* several Jerry Lewis and Dean Martin films and countless Westerns. The newsreel would cover news of the previous week, usually showing Britain from a positive viewpoint, and sports events.

The evening's entertainment was improved when the usherettes came round during the interval while the film reels were being changed to sell tubs of ice cream, choc ices and cartons of orange flavoured drinks. Some unusual extra entertainment was provided one evening when the projector overheated and the film melted, causing the colours to run into each other and form a riot of reds, yellows, oranges, greens in every imaginable shape, so bringing that particular film to a sudden end.

From time to time, there would also be uplifting films in the parish hall – usually black and white films with a semi-religious theme from the 40s, or even earlier, like *Boys' Town* with Spencer Tracy and Mickey Rooney, *Going My Way* and *The Bells of St. Mary's*, both of which starred Bing Crosby as a Catholic priest in New York. Sometimes humour would break through as in the series of films about *Don Camillo*, starring the French actor, Fernandel who, as the parish priest of a small town in northern Italy, was constantly quarrelling with the local Communist administration and particularly its leader, the mayor, Peppone, each trying to get an advantage over the other. In spite of this rivalry, which often involved robust fisticuffs, the two were grudgingly, when it really mattered, allies and, indeed, friends.

On Saturdays, it was back to the Villa Cross Picture House for the children's matinees. *Abbott and Costello meet Frankenstein, Abbott and Costello go to Mars, Tarzan, Roy Rogers, Hopalong Cassidy and Francis the Talking Mule* give a flavour of what we watched. But the highlight was the serial which always ended with the hero or heroine trapped in a situation from which it was impossible to escape, though escape he or she always did, even if we had to wait until the following Saturday to see how it happened. Much of the enjoyment came from being able to cheer the hero or boo the villain and especially making loud kissing sounds on the back of your hand during any romantic scenes, none of which you were able to do when watching at normal times during the week when adults were around.

Newspapers

There was a wide choice of newspapers during the 1950s, mostly with a Conservative outlook. *The Times* was the most prestigious and slow to change. Its front page carried no news until 1966 but was given over to small advertisements usually aimed at the "upper classes". The *Daily Express, Daily Mail* and *Daily Telegraph* were also prominent. The *News Chronicle* generally supported the stance of the Liberal Party, as did the *Manchester Guardian*. Few of the papers supported the Labour Party, which could count only on the trade union paper, the *Daily Herald,* with a daily circulation of over a million and a half, and the *Daily Mirror*. In the case of the *Mirror*, this support was not guaranteed.

The *Mirror* was the daily morning paper in our house and it was exceptional. It was written in a clear, simple style but there was nothing else simple about it. Although supposedly written for anyone with a reading age of twelve or over, it never patronised its readers. Unlike today's tabloids, it was a *real* newspaper and not driven by celebrity stories and gossip. Not that it ignored such things – *one* page was given over to *Donald Zec's* Stories of the Stars. Apart from that, it was a campaigning paper for justice and proper treatment for all, especially the working class. Unlike the Trade Union paper, the *Daily Herald*, the *Mirror* did not blindly follow any political party line. Because it was written in a bright and interesting style, it sold between 4 and 5 million copies a day, far ahead of any rival except the *Daily Express*.

The *Mirror's* contributors included *"Cassandra" (William Connor)* who commented fearlessly on current topics, and cartoonists *(Philip) Zec* (brother of Donald) and *Vicky (Victor Weisz)*. Their often vitriolic pen pictures spared no politician. The sports pages were the equal of any other newspaper and the strip cartoon page was unmatched. *Andy Capp* was a supposedly working class character who never seemed to do any work, *Garth* was a time travelling hero who battled villains through the ages. However, probably the most famous strip was *"Jane"*, a very good-looking blonde who had considerable trouble keeping all her clothes on. It didn't seem to matter where she was, in a lift, getting out of a car or wherever, she always managed to get her dress caught in a door or ripped by a nail and would end up wearing only her scanty under-clothes and stockings. *Jane* was especially popular with soldiers during the Second World War when her adventures were said to have raised the morale of the fighting troops more than a little.

The most popular Sunday papers were the *News of the World*, *Sunday Pictorial*, *The People*, *Sunday Express* and *Empire News*, all of which had circulations of over two and a half million. The *News of the World* was the raciest, with the others following in its wake in the search for scandal. We got *The People* and, during its investigations into some scandal or suspicious enterprise, the story (which usually seemed to be witnessed by one of the newspaper's staff) would always finish just before a description of the juiciest part, or as the reporter was being made a dubious offer, with the words: *"At this point your reporter made an excuse and left"*, leaving the reader to finish off the story in his or her own imagination but very little imagination was needed.

1950s Predications

Newspapers and magazines in the 1950s, (particularly American magazines like *Practical Mechanics*) seemed to have an irresistible urge to publish predictions of what life, and especially transportation, would be like twenty or more years into the future. By 1980 or 2000, we were going to be driving cars powered by small atomic engines. We would leave our luxurious skyscraper homes, collect our car from the underground car park and drive to a main road. We would join a short queue and wait no more than a minute or two until there was a space in the traffic when our car would join the flow and connect to an automatic driving system which would take us effortlessly to the point where we wanted to leave the main road, without any need for the driver to do anything but relax. Then, we would disengage from the automatic driving system and turn off onto a secondary road and drive to our destination by the seaside or in the country.

The pictures illustrating this system would show a smiling family group, including the now relaxing driver, reading or playing board games while the car was travelling safely at sixty or seventy miles an hour, separated from the cars in front and behind by a space of no more than two or three yards. Even when he had taken back the manual control of the car on the secondary road, the driver was still smiling because, for most of the journey, he had nothing to do except relax, read or play board games with the children. Interestingly, the children were always well behaved, smiling, and never bored on these trips.

The automatic driving system was usually based on a moving cable in a slot in the road and the car was attached on to the cable by means of what was essentially a sophisticated set of grippers or clamps.

Levitating trains would speed us at 200 mph or more on longer journeys in unimaginable (for the fifties) smoothness. Even longer journeys would be undertaken by rocket planes. London to New York in an hour and a half, to Australia in five hours. All passengers (not just first class) would sit in comfort and have plenty of room. Travel from the city centre to the airport would be by ultra quiet helicopters.

The launching by the Russians in 1957 of the first artificial satellite, Sputnik, followed by the first manned space flights by Yuri Gagarin and, later, John Glenn led not just to a space race between the Soviet Union and the United States but also to a spate of predictions concerning space travel. The American drive to put men on the moon led to many spin-offs, especially in communications. The Telstar satellite was the start of a revolution in telecommunications. Even so, for a long time to come, international calls had to be pre-booked and made through the operator. The operator was also necessary if you wanted to make for a long distance call between towns. Nowadays, of course, anyone can have instant connections to anyone anywhere in the world.

By 1980, Man would have conquered Space and by the year 2000, thousands, perhaps millions of tourists would be regularly travelling to the Moon or Mars in comfortable spaceships. These tourists would not need any special training nor would they need to be super fit. Couples (married, of course) would fly to the Moon for a long weekend's break and stay in holiday resorts under giant transparent domes where they could walk about as easily as on earth – or even more easily because of the lower gravity on the moon. If they wanted to explore, they would be able to move around the lunar surface in comfortable space suits that were little more than frogmen's suits with helmets, unlike the awkward and bulky space suits that have actually been developed for real astronauts. Mars was too far away for a short break but summer or winter holidaymakers would be thinking of next year's holiday there. The other planets would still be out of reach, except for Government sponsored explorations.

For getting around the modernistic cities, we would have our own individual heli-pack or rocket pack which would fly us swiftly across town at a height of maybe fifty or a hundred feet. Somehow, the problem of bad car drivers on the roads was no longer going to be a problem when these same drivers got out of their cars, slipped on their harness and took to the skies! One type of obstacle all these rocketeers would have to be aware of was the glass covered skyways which would connect the hundreds of residential and office skyscrapers at heights varying from two hundred to over a thousand feet above the ground.

Some of these predictions are now beginning to come to pass in the second decade of the 21st century – long after they were envisaged in the fifties as being operative. Magnetic levitating (*maglev*) trains do exist, with one line operating in Shanghai and another in Japan and others have operated at Birmingham airport, in Berlin and a couple of other places. All lines outside China and Japan have closed down as being too expensive.

Self-driving cars are being developed by BMW and Google, among others, but are still very much in the development stage. They do not have miniature atomic engines although the power for electric and hybrid cars may be produced by nuclear power stations. Nor do they clamp on to a moving cable in the road surface. Instead, they need powerful and sophisticated computer systems to control each individual car. No one seems to have worked out how to cope in the event of a sudden computer crash leading to a real crash. At least in the 1950s prediction, if the cable snapped or jammed, all the cars locked on to it would stop automatically and the drivers would have time to take manual control before continuing their journey.

As for transatlantic flights in less than one and a half hours, weekend breaks on the moon and affordable personal jet packs, all these are still in the realms of fantasy and seem likely to stay there for many years to come – if, indeed, they ever come to reality. One development which did materialise was the *Fairey Rotodyne* – a combination of helicopter/gyrocopter and conventional plane which was designed to take passengers directly from city centre to city centre. A helicopter rotor was used for vertical take off and landing and conventional turboprops were used for level flight. The Rotodyne made 350 test flights, including 230 transitions between vertical and level flight but it proved too costly for development in the fifties and too noisy, so the programme was scrapped. Interestingly, there are a number of projects based on the principles of the Rotodyne now being developed or under consideration.

Another favourite prediction was that most of the drudgery of working in factories and the home would be done by robot labour saving devices. This is one prediction, which has become largely true, whether by robot welders in car factories or dishwashers and other appliances in the home. What, unfortunately, has not become true is the second part of this particular 1950s prediction. These robots were supposed to mean that the amount of work which used to take a working week of 48 or more hours would in future take only 25 hours or even less, thus leaving ample time for sport, recreation or creative activities. Everyone would have ample leisure time together with an increased standard of living. It is true that almost everyone has a higher standard of living than did people in the fifties but the work which remains has not been spread around equally as envisaged then. Instead, many people are working between 35 hours and up to 48 hours a week (still) but many people have no work at all and are trapped in poverty.

Inequality has increased since the days when these predictions were made and this has led to an increase in the gap between the "haves" who still have a job and the "have-nots, who don't. The difference between the 1950s and now is that most people were either poor or only moderately well off. Now the gap between the poor and the rich is getting bigger and becoming reminiscent of Victorian times.

Many of the most common jobs of the 1950s and 60s have been destroyed by the increasing use of robots and, later, computers. Then, every medium size and large company or organisation had its typing pool comprising several, or even dozens of, women who produced all the paperwork needed for a company to operate efficiently. Even small firms had one or more highly trained typists. Typing was very definitely a woman's job, unless you were a go ahead news reporter (and even those recorded most of their reports in shorthand in notebooks). Shorthand typists would transfer the squiggles and abbreviations of shorthand into clear typescripts for presentation to management. Audio typists were even more sought after as they could take what the boss had dictated into a *Dictaphone* and have it typed up, properly punctuated, within minutes. Copy typists could read what had been handwritten and type the copy rapidly and correctly without looking at the keyboard (unlike me as I type out these pages).

These typists used a mechanical or electrical typewriter (the latter was essentially a powered and less tiring to use version of the former and not to be confused with the later *electronic* typewriter with its added features. The skills needed by typists were speed and accuracy of typing as mistakes were laborious to correct.

Any typing pool would be dominated by the sound of clicking keys, the *ping* of the bell to signify that the moveable carriage which held the paper was coming to the end of a line and the rasping sound of the carriage being moved manually to the left, ready to start on the next line. Most of these typist jobs, with their distinctive sounds have now gone, as people are expected to be able to type their own copy on a computer.

Many other office jobs have been taken over by supposedly more efficient computer systems. One which particularly irks me is in the banking system. Fifty years ago, you could pay a cheque into your local bank branch and it would be cleared within five days by a manual postal system and clerks who would physically confirm each cheque and record it manually in a ledger. Today, with all the instant communication of computers, it still takes five days for a cheque to be cleared. Progress???

Millions of other jobs, mostly manual, have also been lost, whether in car factories where assembly work is mostly done by robots or in ports where dockers numbers have been drastically cut due to increased use of containers or on ships which can now be sailed with a crew of less than a dozen instead of double or three times that number of sailors in the 1950s and 60s.

Most of these lost jobs were ones which did not need degrees but which were learned by getting experience on the job. What effort is being made into creating such jobs for today's young people who are not academically minded? We seem to have entered an age when having a piece of paper is the only way you can prove that you are qualified when in fact often the best training is experience and paper qualifications can, in fact, hide actual incompetence.

Smog

Back to the reality of the fifties. One of the most obvious differences between city life in the 1940s and 1950s and today is that the towns and cities then were much dirtier than now. The reason was that almost all houses depended on open coal fires for heating. Tens or hundreds of thousands of open fires burning millions of tons of coal annually made the atmosphere heavy with smoke and soot. Added to this were the factories emitting probably as much smoke again.

Public buildings built in white or grey stone at the end of the Victorian era were blackened by fifty or sixty years of smoke and dirt. People coming home from work had little grains of black in the lines on their foreheads and faces, even though they'd gone to work in the morning freshly washed. Clothes were hard to keep clean during winter. Bronchitis from breathing in the smoky atmosphere was common. But the thing that anyone who grew up or worked in a city in those times remembers is *smog*.

Smog was a regular occurrence each winter and was a mixture of smoke and fog. It was described by Dickens and other Victorian writers as a *"pea-souper"* or *"London Peculiar"* but it happened in every large town and city. Smog was unpleasant to breathe and respiratory illnesses like asthma and lung problems were common.

Smog also played havoc with transport systems. Towns and cities would be brought almost to a halt because traffic could only crawl along streets. During the worst smogs bus drivers depended on their conductors to walk in front of the bus shining a torch so that they could judge where the road ended and the pavement began. It was common for passengers to get off their bus and walk two or three miles quicker than the bus could travel.

Usually, the smog lasted only a day or two but sometimes remained for over a week and many winters would have several such periods. The problem of smog only started to be solved when the burning of ordinary bituminous household coal began to be banned in cities and towns during the late 1950s.

From Primary To Secondary School

In the summer of 1954, during my last term in primary school, I was running in the final of the hundred yards race in the Catholic Junior Sports. Most of the Catholic primary schools in and around Birmingham took part. About eight of the best runners from these schools were in this race. I got the best start of all the runners and was leading all the way until, at about seventy yards, I could see out of the corner of my eye someone overtaking me on the right. At ninety yards, the same thing happened on the left. I came third and was most upset to discover that only the first two runners got medals! Also in that year I passed the eleven-plus exam, which decided what type of secondary school I would attend, and started at St. Philip's Grammar School for boys in Birmingham.

On my first day at St. Philip's, I was not at all pleased to find that both those runners were in my year and two others, equally good, who did not enter that race were also in my class! By the way, one of those last two was Don McLean, who later became a well known comedian and radio and television presenter for his appearances in the children's programme *Crackerjack* and later again in BBC Radio 2's *Good Morning Sunday* on Radio 2 which he presented for sixteen years. He was knighted by Pope Benedict in 2012 and is therefore, he claims, entitled to ride a horse up the steps into St. Peter's church in Rome!

State funded grammar schools were part of the reform of education system begun by the 1944 Education Act. Three types of secondary schools were set up; grammar, technical and secondary modern. All three were supposed to be regarded as equal in status as in the German system but that ideal was never achieved and grammar schools were soon regarded as schools for academic or "clever" pupils and the secondary moderns were for the rest because few technical schools were founded. In fact, many pupils who failed the eleven-plus exam could have coped better with a grammar school education than some of those who did pass the exam.

It was the tradition in many grammar schools, following public schools, that new pupils had to undergo an initiation ceremony. At St. Philip's, this involved being introduced to the "Blue Goldfish". The unwary first-former was asked if he had seen this magnificent creature and, when he said "No", he was taken by two or three of the second-formers to the toilets where his head was shoved down the bowl and the water in the cistern flushed over him. I knew one of the school prefects who told me about this custom so, when I was asked if I had seen the blue goldfish, I knew the right answer to give and I lied.

We were soon introduced to subjects unknown to us in the primary school – Physics, Chemistry, Latin and "Manual Instruction". This last was known in every other school as "Wood-work" but, for some reason, not at St. Philips.

The Manual room was nearly sixty feet long and about a third of that in width, with the teacher's demonstration desk at one end. None of my carpentry efforts turned out as well as I hoped but I was able to claim one distinction in this class. One of my classmates and I had a strong difference of opinion - I can't remember what about and we decided to settle the argument with a fight – in the woodwork room – while the class was going on. So, three or four of the boys kept the teacher occupied at one end of the room while the two of us were scrapping at the other end, rolling about on the floor between the work-benches, with about twenty fellow pupils surrounding us and giving fairly quiet encouragement.

After a while, the door opened and the Deputy Headmaster walked in. Seemingly, he didn't even notice the crowd of boys, or the noise of the two of us fighting on the floor but walked straight past us up to talk to the teacher. Of course, the fight ended immediately. We had quite a few "odd" teachers like that, or perhaps a better description was "absent minded". We also had several excellent teachers as well and between the odd ones and the excellent ones, somehow they managed to give us a very good education.

Another teacher whom I remember with considerable affection was our Latin master, Vic Hermolle. His classes were on Tuesdays and Thursdays in the morning. The first ten minutes or so of the Tuesday class was always taken up with discussing the previous evening's episode of *"Journey into Space"* which was the most popular radio programme in the fifties. In fact, it was the last radio programme to have a bigger evening audience than television. However, our first introduction to Vic was not so cultural.

At St. Philip's, the teachers moved from class to class, while the pupils stayed in the same room, except for practical classes. There we were, thirty-five twelve year-olds, noisy and letting off steam in the short interval between one teacher leaving the classroom and the next one entering. Vic Hermolle entered and stood at the front of the class, waiting for the noise to stop. When it eventually did, he started talking very quietly welcoming us to the joys of Latin which he hoped we would learn to appreciate. He also hoped that we would behave ourselves because bad or inattentive behaviour would upset him.

By this time, we had our new teacher marked out as an easy touch and were nearly hugging ourselves with delight. He paid no attention to our mirth but said simply that, if he got upset, his friend also got upset because it meant that he (the friend) had to do some work. At this, he put his hand into his long black gown and drew out his "friend" which he called his *baculum curvatum* or, in English, "curved stick". It was one piece of the back of a carved chair. The class went quiet and watched in silent awe as Vic calmly explained how the curve of the stick meant that it fitted nicely around a boy's backside and so, unlike a cane, thoughtfully provided a continuous band of pain to anyone on whom it was used! In our three years of Latin classes, I only remember the *baculum* being used twice.

Corporal punishment was used throughout the school, although it was not an everyday affair. Only the Headmaster and his deputy would use the cane. Other teachers usually used a gym shoe or slipper. Everyone accepted the occasional use of the slipper and, on at least one occasion when someone misbehaved and wouldn't own up, our entire class was slippered on the hand. The teacher's rationale was (a) the culprit was not going to get away with his crime and (b) some of the other boys in the class knew who the culprit was but wouldn't tell. Not one boy even considered refusing to hold his hand out for the punishment.

Vic Hermolle also remains in my memory for his claim that, for part of his service in the Second World War, he was one quarter of the air defences of the Northwest frontier of India, then part of the British Empire. Whatever about the truth of that claim, he was the Officer Commanding the school's Air Training Corps, which many of the older pupils joined. The ATC held an annual initiative test and, on one occasion, the test was to see how far the cadets could travel with only a ten-shilling note (50p). One enterprising

17-year-old cadet took himself off to an RAF base and managed to hitch a ride on a transport plane to Malta. His exploit was duly noted at morning assembly but with a reminder that it didn't mean taking days off school was to be encouraged.

"Creamy" Kiernan, our history teacher, was another character. He was short and fat - due, we were firmly convinced, to his habit of going to Pattison's cake shop a few doors from the school every morning break. He called everybody "John" and started every lesson, summer or winter, demanding that someone open a window because "it smells like a Russian Army sock depot in here", or some other memorable but, perhaps, less printable description.

Our English teacher, "Sarky" Sutherland somehow learned of my interest in collecting old and foreign coins. He gave me a number of coins and banknotes, the coins being mostly old English ones and the bank notes being all foreign. One of the coins was a George III crown (5 shillings) which ended up over ten years later as the genuine silver I presented to my bride together with her gold ring (*"This gold and silver I thee give and with all my worldly goods I thee endow"* - not that I had much in the way of worldly goods to endow). I thought I had struck it rich when I went through the foreign banknotes and found I had a beautifully engraved 20,000 mark German note. I was brought back to earth with a bump when I discovered that my fortune was issued during the German hyperinflation of 1923 and that my 20,000 marks were worth less than a penny.

The Headmaster at St. Philip's, Mr T. J. Larkin, was an imposing figure best treated as a sleeping lion that you did not want to wake up! He led the school assembly every day and apart from that, the only times we saw him were for the term reports. If you met him at close quarters at other times, it was usually because you were in trouble. At the end of each term, he would come into the classroom, read your report and tell you what he thought about your efforts in front of the rest of the class. When you got to the fifth form, you had the right to hear his remarks about you in his study, in private. I never worked out which type of interview was worse – the one where your classmates could hear what he thought of your efforts, or the one where you waited outside his door to be told in private.

I do know that waiting outside his study while he gave his opinion of someone else was very similar to waiting in the dentist's waiting room. I remember him asking me in his study what I wanted to do when I left school. With the confident stupidity of a sixteen year old brought up on adventure stories in the *"Eagle"* comic and tales of adventure on the Spanish Main, I answered *"I want to be an explorer, Sir."* Looking back on that incident, I think the most impressive thing about it was that he kept a straight face as he said, *"Well, you'd better make sure to concentrate on your Geography, then"*. And that was his only comment.

One thing which I remember clearly about my time at St. Philip's was the school dinner. Most of the pupils ate these with varying degrees of relish or reluctance. Shepherd's pie, mashed potatoes and braised beef (tough and fatty) were among the staples. For some strange reason, there was usually a slightly soapy taste to the mashed potatoes. But the culinary masterpieces were the deserts (for another strange reason, always served up on plates, not dishes, with thin custard), especially spotted dick and treacle puddings (*"stick to the sides and fill you up"*), chocolate concrete, so called because it was so hard that when you dug your spoon into it, it would split into pieces which would shoot off the plate and onto the floor in different directions. However, the most memorable dessert was rice pudding. This was so thick that I once watched the boy in front of me in the queue slowly turn his plate over and hold it upside down for at least three seconds and the rice pudding remained stuck to the plate with no sign of it being about to fall off.

In The Playground

There were about 700 pupils, all boys, when I attended St. Philip's between 1954 and 1961. The playground was comfortably big enough for about 500, so it was always fairly full. This did not prevent several games of football or cricket (depending on the season) taking place at the same time. This involved keeping your eyes open and your wits about you, otherwise you could get hit unexpectedly by a ball from one or other of the neighbouring games. During the frosty winter months, the playground would be taken over by more than a dozen ice slides, often twenty or more yards long, usually crossing the path of at least one other slide and, in many cases, two or three. Each group of sliders would take a run and slide as fast and far as possible with little attention paid to the other sliders hurtling down their own slide. This sometimes led to collisions and piles of bodies slipping about the place. Amazingly, no one ever seemed to get seriously injured, although the same could not always be said for knees, which were vulnerable in the short trousers we had to wear for the first two years of our secondary schooling. However, injured knees could provide the compensation of a scab forming over the wound because picking at this scab was one of the notable sensations of childhood.

Another common game was *Polly on the mopstick*. This involved two teams of equal size, usually eight to ten boys. One team had one of its members stand with his back against a wall, usually the Oratory church wall if you could find a space among all the competing games. The rest of the team made a line (*the mopstick*) with each boy bending over as for leapfrog. The role of the standing boy was to prevent the head of the first boy in the

133

mopstick from hitting the wall. The other team then took it in turns to leapfrog as far as possible on to the mopstick. When all the team have leaped on to the mopstick, they rocked from side to side and tried to collapse it within a count to ten. If they succeeded, they got another go. Otherwise, the teams changed places and so it went on. One of the unwritten rules was that you had to start off by leaping as far along the mopstick as possible, rather than unfairly pile everyone on top of the first few boys in the line. I don't remember anyone getting permanently damaged, even though collapses of the mopstick were common.

The younger pupils would often be found careering around the playground in our own version of *"British Bulldog"* or *"Hot Rice"*. British Bulldog was never called that but I cannot now remember the name we had for it. In our version, one boy started of as the chaser of the other ten or twelve players. When he caught someone, the two would hold hands and continue the chase. That was straightforward. When another boy was caught, he joined the hand-holding chain and things became slightly more complicated. When the line got close to a group of players, the two boys on the outside frequently decided go after two different targets and confusion arose. Eventually, someone else was caught and the chasing line was split into two twos and the game continued.

Hot Rice was another chasing game but the chaser used a tennis ball to capture another player. The quarry could be hit anywhere on the front of the body, below the neck, and his only way of protecting himself was to hit the ball away with a closed fist. Anywhere on the legs below the knees was a legitimate target area and boys getting out of the way of a low flying ball often made leaps worthy of a high jumper or the principal male dancer in the Bolshoi Ballet company.

A popular all-year round game in the playground with all ages was *Fives,* a form of handball, simplified and adapted to our own rules. Although there was a proper Fives court, similar to that in Eton Fives, almost all games were played against the high flat side wall of the Oratory church. The wall was divided into several playing areas by drainpipes and there was a horizontal line formed by an architectural projection about three feet off the ground. The tennis ball used in the game had to be hit against the wall between the drainpipes and above the three-foot high line. The ball could only hit the ground once before your opponent had to hit it back against the wall. Games were scored like table tennis and would last fifteen minutes or more when evenly matched single or doubles opponents were playing. Of course, several matches were played along the length of the Oratory wall, together with a couple of games of cricket where the wicket was chalked on the wall, so there was plenty of scope to get mixed up with one or two other games, as well as your own.

A lot of the games played depended on unwritten but accepted standards of fairness and this idea was quietly taught in all aspects of the school, the motto of which was *"Pietas"*. This meant not *"piety"* in the modern sense but, more accurately, *"virtue"* which included being loyal and doing one's duty to God, one's family – especially one's parents – and to other people - particularly women - and respecting all these and one's country.

Bad language was strictly discouraged and especially so in the presence of women. We were expected to treat girls and women politely, to hold doors open for them and to walk on the outside of pavements or, if there were no pavements, to walk outside them, nearest to the oncoming traffic so that they would be protected from injury or mud splashes. In other words, we were expected to treat women, young or old, as ladies. Compared to today, what a strange world we were brought up in and what strange expectations of proper behaviour! Or were they?

Sports in School

St. Philip's school was unashamedly academic but it did not neglect the motto of *mens sana in corpore sano (a healthy mind in a healthy body)* and games and physical education or PT (physical *training*) were important parts of our week. We had two PT lessons a week and a full afternoon each week at the school playing field and my favourite sports were both summer ones – athletics and cricket. I was a reasonable long jumper and my sprinting was good enough to get into the relay team for the Joint Sports in my second year. The Joint Sports were an athletic competition involving all the grammar schools in the Birmingham area and the competitive spirit was fierce. I remember two things in particular about the 4 x 100 yard relay race.

I was picked as the fourth member of the team and, considered as one of the weaker runners, I was third in the running order, with the two best runners first and last. As I took over the baton, we were in fifth position out of six teams. The cheering of the spectators from the various schools was loud and constant. I got a very good baton hand-over and started to catch up on the runners in front of me. As I did so, out of the undifferentiated spectator noise, I could plainly hear *"Come on, Rice, come on, Rice!"* I have often wondered since, how I was able to clearly hear this encouragement out of all the indistinguishable racket and yelling going on. By the way, I had pulled up two places into third position by the time I passed on the baton. Our last runner pulled up into second place but we did not progress to the final because we were not the fastest second.

The second thing I remember was how good our baton changing technique was. During our training sessions we got to know exactly how fast our team mates could run and we marked a point on the track so many yards before the start of our hand-over box as the point where, when the runner before us reached it, we would start running as fast as we could, facing straight ahead in the inner side of the lane, with the right hand stretched behind us and thumb and fingers making an upside down v-shape. It was the job of the first runner, holding the baton in his left hand and running slightly outside the receiver, to slam the baton up into that v-shape whereupon the receiving runner closed his hand on the baton and took it away, switching it to his left hand in the first few strides. This technique was aimed at ensuring both runners were going at their fastest at the point of hand-over and, with both runners' arms outstretched it meant an extra yard and a half advantage in each relay sector.

When I watch relay sprints today on the television, I am amazed at how often many of the runners, even at Olympic level, cannot pass over the baton as well as we could when we were only twelve or thirteen years old and how many of them use an inferior hand-over technique which often leads to the receiving runner waving his hand about, trying to reach the baton from a team mate who has almost overtaken him.

At cricket, I was a better than average bowler but by no means brilliant. However, I was good enough in my last couple of years at St. Philip's to be the opening bowler of the 2nd eleven. My role models were the explosive opening fast bowlers of the English and Australian Test teams of the 1950s – particularly Fred Trueman and Ray Lindwall - and I imagined myself (nearly) as fast as them, although in reality, I was very much a medium paced bowler.

In 1961, I set a bowling record of taking seven wickets for three runs during an away match. This impressive sounding feat was due to some considerable extent to a small ridge which ran just slightly left of the middle of the pitch, about five yards in front of the batting crease. For my first wicket, I bowled my usual medium paced in-swinger. The ball hit the ridge and, unusually for my style of bowling, swung out. The batsman gave an almighty swipe, which would have sent the ball for six, if he had connected. He missed, the ball swung back in from the effect of the seam (my original intention) and hit the middle stump, having actually travelled in an arc *around* the bat. I stood staring at the wicket, almost unable to believe my eyes. Then I managed to do the same thing several more times.

During the winter and spring terms, I was a fairly mediocre footballer but when I reached the Sixth Form, one of my friends was captain of the cross-country team. He never had a full complement of runners for the two school teams and every Wednesday morning, the first period of our double maths lesson was taken up with him trying to persuade me to run in the second team. I always refused but, by the end of the period, he had persuaded me to run and we spent the second of the two maths periods trying to find out what we hadn't listened to in the first. I failed my maths "A" level exam.

To sum up, my attitude to cross country running was about the same as the man who was asked why he kept banging his head against the wall, did he like it? His reply?

"No, I hate it - but it's nice when you stop".

Although hockey was not one of the sports played at St. Philip's, on one occasion in the Sixth Form we played a match against the girls of the nearby St. Paul's Grammar school. Expecting an easy victory, we were surprised by the ferocity of our opponents and humiliated by the result. We just did not realise how vicious seventeen and eighteen-year-old girls could be once they had a hockey stick in their hands. Behaving like gentlemen and restricting our advantage in strength and (sometimes) speed only led to hacked shins (we had foolishly assumed that the hockey sticks were for hitting the ball) and writhing in agony on the ground while the girls expertly dribbled the ball several times into our net.

Many of these girls were the same girls who behaved in such a lady-like manner at the joint dancing lessons held after school each Friday to the music of Victor Sylvester and Edmundo Ros! Needless to say, after our complete defeat, there wasn't much enthusiasm for a return hockey fixture with the girls, although we were still happy enough to learn to waltz, quickstep and cha cha cha with them on Friday evenings.

A lot of the senior girls from St Paul's used to attend the daily one o'clock Mass at the Oratory church which was just beside our school and linked to it. As our Sixth Formers were also allowed out at lunch time, there was a surprising upsurge of daily religious devotion among the older pupils and, eventually, quite a number of courtships and marriages resulted from this piety or, as Lonnie Donegan's 1957 song *"Puttin' on the Agony"* expressed it, *"Sweet Sixteen goes to church just to see the boys"*. However, in this case it was more likely for the boys to go to church just to see the girls.

Altar Servers

The Oratory church had a large influence on our secondary education. St. Philip's was set up by Cardinal Newman (an influential member of the Church of England before he converted to Catholicism and founded the Oratory Congregation in Birmingham/Edgebaston) in 1887 and the priests of the Oratory were governors and trustees of the school and some of them taught us.

The part of Birmingham in which I lived had quite a large Irish population and the local Catholic parish, St. Francis's, had a congregation split roughly half and half between English and Irish. Relations were good, as were those with the non-Catholic majority, although my father remembered that, in the forties and early fifties, you could have seen notices for rooms to let with the note "No Irish or Blacks need apply". Apart from the usual name calling among children going to different schools, there was little friction.

For most of my time at primary and secondary school and until I left home to go to College in Twickenham, I was an altar server at St. Francis's. The (all male) choir was very good and, unusually for a Catholic church in the 1950s, had four sections – trebles, tenors, altos and bass. The men in the choir were a cross-section of working class Birmingham. The choirmaster and the lead tenor were both toolmakers in two of the factories which were found all over Birmingham and the Midlands at the time. Most of the adult choir members were manual workers or shop workers. The boys in the choir were paid half a crown (12 and a half pence) a month but the altar boys got no wage. I was quite a good singer and the choir master was always trying to get me to join the choir but I always refused, even though he offered me four times the going rate.

There was considerable rivalry between the servers and the choirboys as to which group was best and occasional fights after the evening service on Sundays and, therefore I could not betray my "gang". Also I had high principles and could not be bought for money. But I must admit to another, less noble reason. Servers who were on the list to serve at weddings, as I was, were sure of getting a tip of at least five shillings (twenty-five pence), and sometimes ten shillings, from the Best Man (funerals only paid two shillings). And, for most of the year, I could depend on serving at a wedding at least once a month, or twice or more a month from April to September.

As the choir was in stalls facing each other in front of the altar and in full view of the congregation, its members had to behave with decorum at all times. The Latin anthems and hymns always sounded most impressive. However, everything was not always as it seemed. Part of the tenor section, led by my father's best friend, Jack Cook, sometimes adapted the magnificent anthem for the feast of All Saints from *"Justorum animae, justorum animae"* (The souls of the Just [are in God's hands]) to *"Who stole the marmalade, who stole the marmalade?"* and, as the rest of the choir was singing the correct version, no one in the congregation ever found out.

I enjoyed serving at Mass, particularly at the main High Mass on Sunday, with the choir, the incense and the elaborate ritual. The Latin and English hymns were very uplifting but there were also more down to earth moments. One of the main servers at High Mass and *Benediction* (the evening service) was the *thurifer* who carried the *thurible* or censer containing burning charcoal and incense. The point of this was that the smoke and incense smell going up to the roof symbolised our prayers going up to God. So that the charcoal would continue to smoulder and send the smell of the incense through the church, it was necessary to swing the thurible from side to side on its chain. This often happened when the thurifer was kneeling. Sometimes the swinging was too vigorous and sometimes young arms got tired and the bowl of the thurible hit the ground, spilling hot charcoal onto the carpet. The carpet in our church had several burn holes created over the years in this way and many an altar boy got scorched fingers from hastily shovelling the hot charcoal back into the bowl of the thurible.

During Easter and Christmas, the main ceremony was Midnight Mass, which started actually at midnight and not at some earlier time as is usually the case now. Of course, the younger servers were normally in bed long before midnight and occasionally one would begin to fall asleep while kneeling with one of the ceremonial candles, to be woken up by one of the older servers hitting the drooping head to stop the hair from singeing when it got too near the flame of the candle. No one ever suffered anything more than a slight embarrassment.

At Christmas Midnight Mass, there would sometimes be a few people who had already started to celebrate the festive season in the pub and I remember in particular one year when the parish priest was wishing the congregation a happy Christmas just before the end of Mass. One of the early celebrators called out in a somewhat unsteady voice *"Thank you, Father and the same to you!"* only to be unceremoniously ejected by a couple of the Churchwardens. I still think the man (who had not caused any disturbance) was only expressing a wish that we all claimed to share and that he should not have been forced out. In fact I have a feeling that the Good Lord has a soft spot for those who are just *slightly* merry. After all, He performed His first miracle when the wine ran out at the Marriage Feast of Cana.

Just opposite the church was (and is) St. Mary's convent where I served Sunday Mass for several years, starting when I was about nine. Going into the convent was entering a world of nuns, holiness, cleanliness and floor polish. Going out after Mass meant leaving these but also the smell of breakfast, with bacon and coffee. I thought these were among the most heavenly of smells. At the time, the only coffee in our house was *"Camp"* liquid coffee and chicory essence in a bottle. It was very strong to my taste, no matter how it was diluted and, in my view, only just about suitable for flavouring icing on cakes. The coffee in the convent was from another dimension altogether. Every Sunday, I longed for the wonderful bacon and coffee. Even though I was going home to a full fried breakfast, this did not compare in my mind to what I was leaving behind.

Imagine my joy when I went to serve my first Christmas Mass at the convent. The nun in charge told me that I was to stay after Mass and have breakfast with the priest because the service normally held in the evening would take place after breakfast, so that the nuns could have the rest of Christmas Day free. I am sure that my ten-year-old mind was thinking more about the breakfast to come than the prayers at Mass!

After Mass had finished, I was shown into the breakfast room with the priest. I was almost dribbling in anticipation of the bacon and coffee. Imagine my shock and disappointment when I saw the table laid with a beautiful breakfast of *cooked turkey and ham, tomatoes, boiled eggs and various types of bread!* In all the seven or eight years I served Christmas and Easter Mass at the convent, that remained the breakfast and I never did get to taste the reality behind the heavenly smells of fried bacon and real coffee.

One thing I should mention, and I regret that it seems to be necessary, is that, during the eleven years or so that I was an altar server before I left home to go to college in Twickenham, I never saw or heard the slightest evidence that any of the priests in the parish were behaving in anything but the most proper way towards the altar servers and choirboys (there were no girls among either group at that time). Of course, some of the priests were impatient (probably justifiably so, from time to time) or even short tempered but they were a powerful influence for good in our part of Birmingham and in my mind's eye I can still see one of our curates, Father Doona, riding his old fashioned bike around the streets on his visits to the sick of the parish. They were not afraid to point out to their congregation that certain things were right and certain things were wrong and, in general, most people recognised the distinction, even if they didn't always act on it. Unlike today, when it seems that many Christian so-called leaders are scared to make any comment which seems to suggest criticism of any thing which is deemed politically correct.

Leaving School, First Job - And A Blonde

In my last year at St. Philip's, before my eighteenth birthday, I had to decide what I wanted to do when I left school and, in spite of my brave reply to the headmaster about being an explorer, I didn't have an idea about my future. Did I want to go to university, or not? During this last year, several people from different professions came to talk to us sixth-formers, including a youngish Army officer who got a fairly hostile reaction from us. He dealt with our many objections with patience, even if he didn't convince many of us or make many converts from our anti-establishment political ideas.

Another person who came to talk to us was the headmaster of a local secondary modern school who said he would be willing to allow anyone thinking of becoming a teacher to join his staff and try out the teaching profession for a year. I decided to take him up on his offer and, at the beginning of the autumn term in 1961, I became an unqualified student teacher at a rate of £31 13s 4d (£31.66) per month before tax, two-thirds of the pay of a newly qualified teacher and equal to £638 in 2014.

People like me tended to be thrown into the deep end in schools in the early sixties and you either sank or swam. In 1961 I was only two or three years older than some of the pupils I was expected to teach, although most of my classes were in the first three years. I was form teacher of a first year class and that was fine. But I also had Form 3b on my timetable. For some reason, the second stream in the third year was almost always the worst to keep under control in every school I taught in and even experienced teachers could have problems with them. 3b were notorious and I had them for five lessons a week, two of them on Friday afternoon.

I was not the only one who had problems with 3b. A Maths teacher in his thirties with the build of a rugby player had particular difficulty with one boy, called Loughney. On one occasion after several weeks of consistent provocation, the teacher came into the staff room in great glee and told us that he had sent the pupil to get the cane from the headmaster. In his excitement to let us know of his success, he got the name and punishment mixed up as he gleefully announced:

"I've just had Thrashney locked!"

Many of us felt that was the best thing that could have happened to him.

After the first three weeks, I was ready to give up but my father advised me to stick it out for another month and then decide what to do. By the end of the month, I was beginning to enjoy teaching, even if I never looked forward to 3b on Friday afternoon. Another factor in my decision to stay was that I soon began to go out with Rose, a newly qualified teacher who was an attractive blonde and just twenty, only two years older than I was. She was the reason I started to smoke for the first time since my father had made me smoke a cigarette nearly ten years before but that was the only bad habit she led me into.

Our romantic affair really was that – *romantic* – like in a Sandra Dee Hollywood film of the time. Sandra Dee was always the typical wholesome girl next door. Going to the pictures with Rose and afterwards sharing a bag of hot roasted chestnuts from a street vendor was a delight. In fact, in those days, even just walking beside a lake near her home with your arm around your girlfriend and hers around you and the street lights in the distance glowing faintly in the deepening twilight, was something very special when you were eighteen and in love!

After smoking lightly for about four years, I gave up the habit completely. Rose also informed me that my tie should always match my socks – a piece of style advice that I still sometimes find myself thinking about, if rarely following, as I search in my sock and tie drawer over fifty years later. We went out together for the year I was teaching at that school but our paths parted when I went to College and shortly afterwards she met her future husband.

I must admit that I got a boost to my ego when I telephoned Rose recently and spoke to her for the first time in nearly forty years to enquire about a mutual former colleague who had died and she told me that she still had two pieces of jewellery I had bought for her all those years ago – a necklace and a brooch.

"I bring them out from time to time to show my grandchildren. I tell them 'You see, I <u>did</u> have a life before I met your grandad!' "

Just as the grammar schools in the Birmingham area had their Joint Sports, so the Catholic secondary schools had the Catholic Sports, held at St. Philip's sports field. During my student teaching year, I was in charge of the boys' long jump event. Now, this is not the event likely to draw the most spectators. However, shortly after the jumping started, one of my 16 year-old pupils came over and asked if she could help, as she had been knocked out of her own event. This girl was one of the most beautiful I have ever seen. She was Anglo-Indian and had lovely amber coloured skin. She was a very nice and sensible girl, without any apparent realisation of how good-looking she was, especially in the shorts and (modest) running vest she was wearing.

I asked her to rake the sand after each jump. Within less than five minutes of her arrival, nearly all the boys who were not then actually involved in an event, and also a very high percentage of the

146

male teachers, had suddenly lost interest in all other events and developed an overpowering one in the boys' long jump. She didn't do much good for the concentration of the boys trying to break the long jump record, either!

Leaving School At Fifteen

Most people were not fortunate enough to stay at school until they were eighteen and then go on to further education. The official minimum school leaving age between 1947 and 1972 was fifteen and until well into the 60s this was the age most people finished their formal education. From then on, there was a gradually increasing number of people who stayed on at school until they were sixteen. However, most people (about seven in every eight) left school without any exam qualifications and started work on building sites or in factories, offices or shops as general assistants, delivery boys, typists or junior office girls, often making tea and doing whatever menial jobs were required. Gradually, they could progress as they gained experience. Quite a few boys would become apprentices following a course which combined on the job practical training with classroom based theoretical knowledge, an opportunity which was not so widely available for girls, except in nursing and perhaps in hairdressing.

One girl's experience

I left Secondary school in Kinver (a small country village in South Staffordshire) in 1962, just after my fifteenth birthday. The school was unusual in that we were taught fencing, something I enjoyed very much. As I was the second eldest in a family of seven girls and one boy, I had plenty of experience looking after young children and so I soon got a job as a live-in Nanny looking after a six month old baby in a family who owned a very successful electrical business. I stayed there happily for

about two years, then started training as a Nursery Nurse. After my
two year training and my probationary year, I started another two year
course in Birmingham to train to be a State Enrolled Nurse and I
qualified as such just after my twenty-second birthday.

National Service

I mentioned previously, during my description of going on summer
holiday that there always seemed to be a lot of National Servicemen
travelling on the trains. In the 1950s and up to the start of the 60s,
young men between the ages of 17 and 21 were required to serve for
two years in one of the armed forces unless they were exempted
because of unfitness, studying at university or some other reason.

During the 1950s, national servicemen were called upon to fight
alongside regular soldiers in the Korean War and the "emergencies"
in Kenya against the Mau Mau, in Cyprus against the Greek
Cypriots seeking union with Greece and in Malaya against
communist forces. They also served in Egypt before and during the
Suez Canal "crisis" and in garrisons all over the remaining British
colonies and dependent territories. At the start of the 1950s, the
total number of men serving in the armed forces was just under 1
million. Ten years later, it had shrunk to half that number and
National Service was being phased out.

When I went to College in 1962, one of my fellow students was
among one of the last groups of young men who had done National
Service. He was called up into the Army in 1960. The following
year Kuwait, which had been under British control, became
independent. Iraq, which had long claimed it as part of its national
territory, began preparations to invade Kuwait and reunite it to the
rest of the country. Since Britain still had a defence agreement with
Kuwait, British troops were sent out to defend it against the Iraqi
forces. My fellow student was one of these soldiers and he told us:

"We disembarked from the ship with all our equipment. We were rushed up to the border with Iraq and we dug in to wait for the expected invasion. There we were, supported by tanks, field guns and heavy machine guns and we had our own personal rifles. But we did not have a single shell or bullet for any of them. If the Iraqis had known this and had invaded, the only thing we could have done was to act as traffic policemen for their tanks as they crossed the border!"

I learned about another example of the strange things that went on in the Army when I met Gwyn Jones some years later in Saudi Arabia. Gwyn, a Welshman (obviously) had qualified as a teacher in the early fifties. In 1954 or '55 he applied for a post at a small British Army school in Penang, in Malaya. He was appointed headmaster and given the equivalent rank of Captain, in accordance with his salary, and an officer's house and furniture suitable to his rank. Six months later Penang was chosen as the base for a combined Commonwealth brigade of troops fighting the Communist insurgents in what was called the Malayan "Emergency". Thousands of troops and support units arrived and some were accompanied by their families. This influx meant more children in his school and an increase in salary. However, his increased salary could not be paid to a mere Captain, so he was "promoted" to the equivalent of a Major. All his Captain's furniture was removed and replaced by Major's furniture.

Another few months went by and more and more children arrived at the school, entitling him to a further increase in salary. So he got a further "promotion" to "Colonel" and his Major's furniture was removed and replaced by furniture deemed more appropriate to a Colonel's status. This sort of thing was typical in the Army of the 1950s where attitudes of "class" and colonial thinking persisted even more strongly than in England itself.

Between that first appointment in Penang and 1971, Gwynn never worked for more than a year at a time as a teacher in Britain. The only reason he did this was that, by the time the *Times Educational Supplement* reached him in whatever far-flung part of the British Commonwealth he was in, all the vacancies advertised had been filled and he had to return to Britain to apply for another job abroad. He ended up as Headmaster in a secondary school in Zambia, living in a large bungalow with beautiful gardens and a swimming pool and with servants, car and a large salary all provided.

College Years

In 1962 I applied to enter St. Mary's teacher training College in Strawberry Hill, Twickenham. This was in an idyllic setting, close to the River Thames on the (then) outskirts of southwest London. The college was described as "a sports field surrounded by buildings" and this was fairly accurate, since athletics and sports formed a large part of the study course for the many students training to be P.E. teachers. Several Olympic athletes studied there, perhaps most notably Gordon Pirie, the long distance runner of the 1950s and 60s and Mo Farah, who won both the 5,000 metres and 10,000 metres at the London Olympics in 2012. Many people involved in the theatre and television worlds also studied at St. Mary's; probably the best known of these being the comedian Tom O'Connor.

The most famous of the buildings of the college is Strawberry Hill House, built in the neo-Gothic style by Horace Walpole between 1749 and 1746. It became the model for the design of the Houses of Parliament when they were rebuilt after being destroyed by fire in 1834.

The students who joined in 1962 were the first teaching students to have a three-year course of studies, as opposed to the previous two years. Student numbers increased from 400 the previous year to 600. The college's small size meant that you knew most of the students, at least by sight. I studied (if that is the right word) Education, French, Geography and History. My room-mate, Carl Wylde, whom I had known at grammar school, studied Education, Physical Education and Religious Education and we soon became firm friends in spite of my envy of him. I would have described him at that time as "rugged" rather than handsome, but that did not stop students at women's colleges being apparently irresistibly attracted to him, without any obvious effort on his part. I, however, had to work hard for whatever limited measure of success I had with the opposite sex.

After my year's student teaching when I left school, I had expected to be one of the oldest students in the First Year. In fact, aged nineteen, I was one of the youngest. Many of my fellow students had worked for two, three, or even more years before they decided to go in for teaching.

In 1964, the student whom I mentioned above as having served in Kuwait during his National Service had a stroke of good fortune when he bought a 1939 Riley 12 saloon car. This had been bought new by a wealthy businessman who had three other cars. He died a couple of months later and his widow kept all four cars in running order, or rather her chauffeur did. The widow died in 1964 and left the Riley to the chauffeur. He just wanted rid of it and sold it at a bargain price to my student friend.

The car was immaculate and looked as if it had just been driven out of the showroom. With less than 1,000 miles on the clock in 25 years, an engine that purred when started up and doors that closed with a satisfying *"thud"*, like railway carriage doors, the Riley was a real bargain and was later sold again for a substantial profit.

Perhaps inspired by this, in the summer of 1964, my friend Carl decided to buy an ex-GPO Morris 8 quarter-ton van. He submitted tender offers on three vans, which were for sale as being surplus to the GPO's requirements. His offers were £8, £10 and £12. His offer of £10 (equal to about £170 in 2014) was accepted and he proudly drove his eleven-year-old model Z back to college. It had only three forward gears and on a good day could reach a top speed of about 50 mph. Between 38 mph and 42 mph it shook so violently that we thought it was going to fall apart. This shaking happened all the time between those speeds but below 38 mph and above 42 mph, it functioned normally – or as normally as ever it did.

The windscreen was hinged at the top and could be opened by winding a handle on the dashboard. There was only one windscreen wiper, on the driver's side and it too was hinged at the top. Driving in the rain at a modest pace, the wiper would work normally, giving no hint of what was to come. As the van's speed increased, the wiper would start to restrict its sweep, gradually moving up the right hand half of the screen and sweeping a half and then a quarter of what it should have been wiping.

Eventually, the wiper would give up on the windscreen completely and sweep furiously and totally uselessly in the air above the screen. When this happened, Carl (while still driving) would wind open the windscreen, put his hand through the space created, lean as far forward as he could and reach up for the wandering wiper and pull it down onto the screen again where it would continue to work for perhaps five or ten minutes before the whole process would start again.

Carl's ex-GPO van
Kay Keane

One Saturday in summer, when the coach for the college cricket team did not turn up, Carl's van was pressed into service as the substitute transport. The eleven players and the twelfth man crammed into the back, which was separated from the seats by a strong wire mesh. Carl drove while I sat in the passenger seat where I was forced to have the girlfriend of one of the players on my lap. Unfortunately for me, the journey only lasted about twenty minutes. This was probably just as well because, even in those less regulated days, the police would not have been very happy if they had seen a small ex-GPO van carrying a total of fifteen people. The cricket team lost the match.

During one holiday from college, Carl decided to take the van and tour around North Wales. This proved to be not an entirely wise decision. Going up a narrow mountain road near Snowdon, he found that the top gear (third) could not cope with the slope so naturally he changed down to second and was still slowing. Even first gear could not prevent the van coming to a halt. So, he went up the road in reverse gear, leaning out of the window and pushing against the stonewall bordering the road to help the van on its way. Making slower and slower progress in this way, he was overtaken and passed by two hikers going up the hill on foot.

After our first year, Carl and I were moved out of our room in a college-owned house and into a private house about half a mile away with two other students. We lived there on a bed and breakfast basis. The landlady, a slim and very active 72-year-old widow, did not believe in over-feeding us. Breakfast consisted of a cereal followed by a fry. The fry was either egg, tomato and beans or egg, fish fingers and beans. If we got to college in enough time, we would queue up in the refectory for another, more filling, breakfast.

The refectory could hold about half the students at one time and we had our other meals there, served by "nippies", so called after the waitresses in Lyon's Corner Houses. The food was filling, rather than gourmet. This was not surprising as the Government allowance to the college for each student's food was £1 7s (£1.35p) a week (the equivalent of £25 in 2014), which was less than the allowance to feed a prisoner in one of Her Majesty's prisons. Tea and coffee were served in big urns, which seemed to be swilled out rather than properly washed and it was often difficult to decide whether it was tea or coffee you were getting out of the urn. The other thing I remember clearly was the supper at nine o'clock. This consisted of strong cocoa (made with water, not milk) from one of the same urns and an "oggy". These oggies were large, sticky buns with raisins and they were very popular. Most people tried to get at least a second one to take to the bedroom in case they were attacked during the night by pangs of hunger.

None of the students got fat on the food we had at college but, at least we didn't starve. Well, not too much.

The annual College Rag Week at St Mary's, Strawberry Hill was called, not entirely imaginatively, "Strawberry Fayre". It was very similar to rag weeks in many other colleges and universities and included bed pushes which held up traffic while strangely dressed students pushed collecting tins into the cars of (usually) very patient motorists, students jumping into the River Thames from Richmond Bridge, tours of the historic Strawberry Hill House, barbecues and the Strawberry Ball. The latter was the high point of the College's social calendar and, oddly enough, in the refectory the following day were a number of young ladies who had obviously travelled early to the College in order to sample breakfast with their respective young men!

During our time as students, St. Mary's College (or *Simmaries* as it was colloquially called) was for men only and, perhaps surprisingly, we were quite happy with this. There were several women's colleges within easy travelling distance and at least one dance somewhere most weeks, so there was usually no shortage of places to look for potential female company when finances allowed. When the college became co-educational in the autumn of 1965, most of us who finished our course in the summer of that year were glad we were leaving before the women arrived. We considered that the atmosphere of the college would totally change – and we were right.

If you were going out with a girl, there was nothing more impressive than taking her "into town", that is into central London for a meal at a *proper* restaurant. Of course you had to be pretty keen on the girl to invest the large sum of money required. So, such rare outings depended on them taking place in the first half of a term, before your grant had run out! After all, when the maximum grant was £44 for a term, an evening out "in town" could cost most of a week's share of that.

On one occasion, I took a girl I was anxious to impress to the cinema and then to Lyon's Corner House in the Strand. This was something special for a boy from Birmingham. The Corner Houses were a tradition since 1909 and provided good food at fairly reasonable prices (for London). Each of the Corner Houses had several restaurants.

I remember going downstairs to the third most expensive restaurant of five – *Come on, I* was *only a student!* This had a Continental theme, a minstrel gallery and a four piece "Hungarian Gypsy band". The lead violinist wandered between the tables, playing airs from Viennese operettas for the young (and not so young) lovers. How could any girl not be impressed? This romantic atmosphere was dampened for one couple when a waiter spilled most of her dinner down the girl's dress. We were not the couple involved but it did spoil the ambiance a bit.

Usually, I couldn't afford such extravagance and the most a girl could hope for was a meal in a small, cheaper, but still sophisticated restaurant. I could tell the restaurant was sophisticated because the tables had red and white check tablecloths and there was a candle in an empty wine bottle on each table. But the absolute proof of the sophistication of the restaurant and therefore of the people like me who took a girl there, was the fact that it served *Chianti* with the bottle nestling in a wicker basket. How could anyone handle any more Continental sophistication than that? And, it was a lot cheaper than Lyon's Corner House. Don't forget, this was a time when a fella who asked a girl out on a date expected to pay for the evening - even if he had to borrow some money from her half way through!

Most evenings out were even cheaper, maybe with a session at the college folk music club and a pint or two of beer for me and probably cider for the girl (if I was lucky to be going with one at the time) somewhere locally. I remember one (girl-less) evening when one of my friends said he had heard that a pub in Richmond, just a short train journey from the college, served *Mead*, genuine old English style, the sort that Anglo-Saxons and Vikings used to drink in large quantities. So, five of us set off from college to Richmond and enquired at the first pub we visited if they served mead. The barman told us they didn't but he directed us to another pub, which did. We went in and asked for five pints of mead. What we got were five small glasses, each holding less than a quarter of a pint. The regulars were drinking half pints. I took a sip. The mead was very sweet, being a honey based drink, but pleasant, so I took a bigger sip. Nothing happened at first but, after about ten seconds, I got a hot and prickling sensation inside my head. Then, everything cleared away and my next sip had no effect. All my friends had the same sensation. We had another small glass each. This time, there was only the sweet and pleasant taste.

After that, we left the pub, walked up the road and called in at a café. It happened to be my turn to buy the coffee and buns, so I counted out 7s 4d (37 pence) to pay for them – except that I didn't. It took me four attempts to count out the money before I got the right amount. Yet I was not slurring my speech and I had no feeling of being drunk at all. I've not had mead since.

Mention of the college folk club reminds me of one particular evening. The folk club was very popular, not least because you could invite a girl to it and spend very little money on the date, an important factor as the term went on and the grant money disappeared. On this one particular evening, the club committee had asked Miki and Griff, who lived nearby, to come and sing.

Miki was the female member of the duo. They were a sort of older version of the very glamorous and popular Nina and Frederick and they were both in their early forties at the time, so their appeal to most of the nineteen to twenty-four year olds in the audience was somewhat limited. Their biggest success was *"A little bitty tear let me down"* which got to number 16 in the charts.

They came on after a few of the college folk singers and were received politely, if not overly enthusiastically. Once they started singing however, things changed. It took them less than a minute to have the audience in the palms of their hands. They were so professional in how they brought everyone along with them and they were of a much higher standard than even the best of the other singers. The not overly enthusiastic reception at the start turned into applause and cheers at the end of the first song, repeated requests for more and great reluctance to let them leave at all.

Since we were studying at a Catholic teacher training college, during our first year attendance at Church Music on Fridays was compulsory. As in many other things which were "compulsory" in our college, the definition of this word was highly flexible but these sessions of Church Music were surprisingly popular and about half the two hundred students in First Year would attend each week, even if not necessarily the same students every week. The music was mostly Latin Gregorian plainchant and, if you haven't experienced being part of – or even just hearing - one hundred male voices, some good, some bad but most of them probably indifferent, blending together without any instrumental accompaniment, to produce an impressive performance of *"Dies Irae"* the Latin hymn *"Day of Wrath"* about the Day of Judgement, then you've missed something quite special.

Exams had to be faced and passed every year and sometimes the second part of this requirement was not always straightforward. In his second year, Carl was faced with a paper where he could not answer a single question. So, he took an imaginative step to success. He wrote four essay questions of his own, answered them all adequately and passed the exam.

Living as students, we led a fairly self contained life in college but, on two occasions during my first two years, events in the outside world had dramatic effects on all of us. The first time was in October 1962 when the Cuban missile crisis burst into the world's attention. Earlier in 1962, the United States installed nuclear missiles in Italy and Turkey. These were targeted at Moscow and other Russian cities and were much closer to these targets than other American missiles. In retaliation, the Russians started building launching sites for their own nuclear missiles in Cuba, only 90 miles from Florida. When these preparations were discovered by the American Government, it demanded that the Russians stop work immediately and withdraw all offensive weapons from Cuba.

The Russians refused and sent cargo ships carrying missiles to Cuba. The Americans declared a blockade around Cuba and threatened to fire on any of these ships trying to break the blockade. As the Russian ships neared the American line of blockade, fears grew of hostile action between the ships of the two countries, leading to outright war which was expected to turn into a nuclear conflict.

For about two weeks, the world waited fearfully to see what would happen when the Russian ships met the American navy. Frantic diplomatic efforts were made to resolve the danger but without apparent success. However, secret negotiations eventually led to the Russian ships turning back before they reached the blockade line, work on the missile sites ceasing and the Russians removing their bombers from Cuba. These concessions from the

Soviet Union were followed at a discreet interval by the Americans withdrawing the nuclear missiles, which had started the crisis from Italy and Turkey. The world breathed again.

The second world event which intruded into our lives happened just over a year later, in November 1963. This was the assassination of President John F. Kennedy. The shock which was felt all over the world was enormous because Kennedy was young, handsome and seemed to offer new hope to people in many countries longing for freedom. And now he had been cut down in his prime. At first, many Americans thought the assassination was a plot, either by the Soviet Union in retaliation for the Cuban crisis the year before, or by shadowy figures in the CIA or the Mafia. But, it was none of these and although US military forces went on high alert in case of a Russian attack, they were soon stood down to their normal alert level. At college, lectures were suspended as most students watched the television broadcast of the President's funeral, such was the effect he had had on young people.

As we were training to be teachers, each year we had to do a month's teaching at one of the local, or not so local, schools. My first and final teaching practices were at schools near the College and my second year practice was at a tough secondary school in Whitechapel in London's East End. My final teaching practice showed how much one's life can be affected or even changed by chance or serendipity – or, perhaps, something else entirely.

The other final year student teaching at the same school as me was in line for a distinction, so he had to be assessed by an outside examiner. These examiners checked up on about 20% of the students to ensure that the College lecturers' assessments of their students were accurate. Since the outside examiner would be in the school to assess the quality of my companion's teaching, he took the opportunity to assess my ability, as well.

We knew the lesson, which the examiner would assess but we didn't know the time he would come into the classroom. I was teaching maths to first year class of very keen eleven year olds and enlisted the help of four or five of them to help me get ready for this special lesson. The lesson began with no sign of the examiner arriving. Normally when I would ask a question, there would be at least a dozen hands raised by children eager to give an answer. Now the tension I was feeling must have transmitted itself to my four or five helpers and, through them, to the rest of the class. After a couple of minutes, I asked my first question and got no response. It was as if all the class had been turned into wood.

It was the same with the next question and the next. By the time ten minutes had gone with no improvement, I was beginning to panic. Then one boy, who had been looking for something in his desk, dropped the desk lid with a loud bang. I made some remark which was not at all funny but the class laughed. The tension was broken. I asked another question. Twenty-five hands went up. At that exact moment the door opened and the inspector walked in on an apparently very successful lesson – which it was from then on. Did that happen by chance, or was my Guardian Angel hard at work? Whichever it was, I think most people can recall something similar from their own lives.

A small incident during this third and last year in College shows how much the world has changed during the fifty years since then. One of the older students in my year (he was about twenty-five) became engaged to be married. Although he had been legally an adult for four years, he was still required to ask the Vice-Principal for permission to marry. This permission was not a formality but it was granted. Similar situations were not confined to Catholic colleges but happened in state institutions, too. Up to at least 1969, a nurse who had not completed training to become a State

Registered or State Enrolled Nurse had to get the hospital Matron's permission to get married. If either the College student or the student nurse had got married without getting the required permission, there was the possibility that he or she would not have been allowed to complete their course of training and could not, therefore have qualified as a teacher or nurse.

Hitch Hiking In Ireland And Germany

In 1965, during the summer after we finished college, Carl and I went for a month's hitchhiking in County Donegal and the West of Ireland. The weather was gorgeous as we walked and hitched around the rugged coasts. Among the sights we saw were ancient stone forts, some dating back 2,000 years or more, beautiful and empty golden beaches, basking sharks and seals. We saw the silver streaks of crystal-clear streams tumbling down the slopes of the heather clad mountains and hills. It was beside one of these crystal-clear streams that we pitched our tent one evening below a small ridge.

Carl, who fancied himself as a backwoodsman, started to build a low fireplace with the stones, which lay scattered about, while I went down the hill to gather wood for the fire. After a meal of scorched but (as far as we were concerned) tasty sausages and syrup sandwiches we washed our utensils in the stream and stretched out on the short, springy grass in our sleeping bags and went to sleep.

The next morning, after breakfast and a refreshing wash in the stream. I decided to go exploring. Climbing over the ridge which had sheltered us, I had not gone more than twenty yards before I came across the body of a dead and rotting sheep in the water. Our crystal-clear stream which had provided our water for tea, cleaning the dishes and for washing was, in fact, a stream of germs and pollution!

We soon struck camp and moved on, having learnt to check *up*stream as well as down before selecting our camping spots from then on.

We spent some time on Aranmore Island, about a mile offshore from the small fishing village of Burtonport in the northwest of Ireland, with our tent pitched on the grass- scattered sand dunes just behind the beach itself. One night, I awoke to a sound that I could not recognise. It sounded like some strange animal clearing its throat, followed by a softer sound. As the sound came slowly closer, I tried to think of what it could be. Thoughts of fearsome sea monsters of Irish folklore came, unbidden, to my mind. I put off looking out of the tent for as long as I could, hoping the sound would go away. But no, it came closer and closer to the tent. At last, I nerved myself to peer out of the tent. There it was in the dim light – some kind of huge animal, slowly coming closer to us. As my eyes grew accustomed to the dark, I could see..... an old horse! The rasping, throaty noise was the sound of the coarse beach grass being torn up by the roots and the softer noises came as the horse chewed and swallowed the grass.

A noise that would not have been noticed during the day became amplified and scary in the stillness and silence of an Irish island night.

One other incident comes to mind from that holiday. We had moved on to County Galway, on the west coast and had made good progress hitching on this particular day. Our last lift left us in a remote area along a quiet country road with no walls or hedges separating it from the surrounding rocky countryside. We walked on for quite a while until it became pitch dark and we had to camp for the night. The only flat area was just off the road, so we started to erect the tent. When it came to knocking the tent pegs into the ground, we were surprised to find the soil so hard and stony that we had to drive the pegs in almost horizontally.

Once in the tent, our night passed without incident. When we awoke the next morning, we found the reason for the horizontal tent pegs. We hadn't erected the tent away from the road, as we thought but actually in the middle of a triangular lightly grassed piece formed by the junction between our road and another even smaller road. We had been trying to knock the pegs into the metalled surface of this road junction. The traffic along these two country roads was so slight that not one vehicle had come along during the night – which was just as well for us!

On another occasion, Carl and I decided to hitchhike to the Oktoberfest in Munich to sample the beer there. This was at a time when continental beer was very rare in England. We took the ferry to Ostend and a train from there to Luxembourg, travelling in a third class compartment with surprisingly comfortable wooden seats. From Luxembourg we hitched into Germany without any incident. We were waiting on the entry slip road leading on to one of the autobahns trying to get a lift before we had any problems. We tried unsuccessfully for a lift for over two hours and then got out the map to see if we could find another route when a Citroën DS stopped. The driver spoke to us but we had a problem understanding him because neither of us understood German. However, I did pick out one word from what he said and that was the name of a city which I knew was on our route – Karlsruhe. So I said "Ja" and we got in.

The Citroën DS was one of the most futuristic cars of its time, with advanced *hydropneumatic* suspension which gave by far the smoothest ride of any car of the time and a beautiful aerodynamic shape which attracted admiring looks wherever it went.

The driver, probably in his early thirties spoke to us again in German but we used up almost our entire vocabulary with: *"Wir sprechen kein Deutsch" (We don't speak German")* and so Carl and I sat chatting together for the next twenty minutes until our driver started to speak perfect English, having obviously listened to and understood everything we had said to each other. He took us over two hundred miles in just two hours forty-five minutes, including eighty miles through thick fog where his speed never dropped below 60 mph, even though the visibility in places was less than twenty yards. I was never so glad to get out of a car.

We were now out of the fog and our next lift took us into the Black Forest in southwestern Germany just as the daylight was fading. The driver left us on a local road near his home and we waited as the evening turned into a moonless night. At this point, the road cut through a dense part of the forest with trees coming right to the edge of the road on both sides. There was very little traffic and we could hear the sounds of the wind rustling in the trees, of owls hooting, bats sweeping past us and dogs or foxes howling in the distance. It was quite eerie and it was not hard to see how people were afraid of what was to be found in the forests when most of Europe was covered with dense forests and wild animals lurked in them.

I have already mentioned that the stories of fairies in Ireland are distorted memories of ancient, pre-Celtic people. Here in the Black Forest in the dark, it was easy to picture the background reality to the stories in Grimm's Fairy Tales where travellers could get lost for days or weeks and children were warned by these fairy tales to keep out of the forests because of the dangers they contained. When these tales originated, in versions much darker and frightening than the Disneyfied tales children learn today, most of Europe was covered by forests with scattered villages in clearings. Beyond the fields of these villages wild animals such as bears, wild boars and wolves lived and were to be avoided. Goldilocks and Red Riding Hood were lucky that they were not killed by the three bears or the wolf.

After some time, we got a lift to the nearest village where we got a room for the night but we never did get to the Oktoberfest, or Bavaria, although we did sample some excellent local beers before we headed back to England. Coincidently, about the time we made this journey, a German pianist, Horst Jankowski, had a number 3 Top Ten hit in Britain with his instrumental piece *"A Walk in the Black Forest"*.

PART TWO

Going Out With A Second Blonde, Being Dumped and An Offer I Couldn't Refuse

After I finished my teacher training in 1965, I started teaching in Blessed (now Saint) John Wall Secondary Modern school in Handsworth Wood, a pleasant suburb of Birmingham. It was a small, mixed school with only about 300 pupils. It shared playing fields on a site of nearly twenty acres with Handsworth Technical School. Beyond the school playing fields was a golf course, so it was almost like being out in the country. The drawback was that the grounds were alongside the River Tame and were very low-lying. During winter and spring, a large part of the playing fields was flooded, to such an extent that the members of the school canoe club could paddle their canoes through the soccer pitch's goalposts.

One other newly qualified teacher started at the same time as me – Di, the girls' P.E. teacher - again, an attractive blonde. As we were the youngest members of staff, we started going out together. I enjoyed her company and I hope she enjoyed mine - she did at least give the impression of doing so. Neither of us regarded our relationship as one which was likely to lead to anything serious in the long term and so it proved. Di and I were together one evening shortly after the New Year in 1966 when she surprised me by asking would I mind if we stopped going out together, as she had met someone whom she liked a lot (enough, in fact, to marry him later). We had always known something like this would happen sooner or later, so I agreed and we remained friends. This took place on a Monday evening.

The following evening, my school and college friend, Carl, came to my parents' house and asked me:

"How do you feel about going round the world?"

As I was still feeling sore about being dumped, even if gently, I gave the only possible answer -

"That's a great idea. Let's do just that."

Those two questions, within twenty-four hours of each other, and my replies to each of them were eventually to change the course of my life although I had no idea of this at the time.

The next day, Wednesday, we borrowed £300 (more than two month's combined net pay for two newly qualified teachers and worth about £5,000 in 2014) from Carl's mother and on Saturday we bought a 1956 model soft top short wheel base series I Land Rover - the sort where the headlamps were placed inside the front wheel wings just in front of the radiator grill. Carl would have preferred to buy an Austin Champ - a jeep-like vehicle produced for the army. The Champ was designed as a go anywhere vehicle for four people - it could even be driven in water up to six feet deep when a snorkel tube was fitted and it could travel as fast in reverse as forward, up to 60 mph. However practical reasons made us opt for the Land Rover. The Land Rover could carry more cargo, it was less heavy on fuel and it was easier to maintain mechanically.

If we had had to save up the money to buy the Land Rover, I think we would have given up on the idea but, having bought the Land Rover, we had to do something with it. In fact, it took us nine months to pay the £300 back, get the Land Rover ready, and save enough to finance our trip.

Our first task was to make sure the Land Rover was in good enough condition for the journey, which very soon changed from going around the world to going around Africa, so we bought the official workshop manual which was about eight times the thickness of the owner's manual. We stripped down everything that could be stripped down, checked everything for wear and replaced what needed replacing, cleaned everything that could be cleaned and generally did all that we could to get our vehicle in tip top condition. Wherever the workshop manual said to unscrew six screws, we unscrewed six screws; wherever it said to tighten up ten screws, we tightened up ten screws. We followed all the manual's instructions to the letter. When we finished, we had more than twenty screws left over!

Preparing the Land Rover

We bought spares for every thing, including shock absorbers and springs. The Land Rover had a 12 gallon fuel tank. We fitted a second, 30 gallon tank and carried two 5 gallon jerrycans. In all we could carry enough petrol to see us through more than 600 - 700 miles of rough driving. We had two complete sets of five tyres – road tyres for travelling through Europe and off-road tyres for Africa. We had sand ladders and a spade to help dig us out when we were stuck in soft sand. We built wooden lockers to keep our belongings safe and we even had an inflatable rubber boat for when we were in tropical central Africa and fancied a bit of river exploring!

From left to right, myself, Carl and Carl's mother (our banker) and the Land Rover with the cross country tyres on the roof

We had the best maps available – Michelin maps which showed the recognised stopping places and where water was available, how deep the well was and whether the water was good, drinkable or brackish. We had sterilising tablets to make sure the water would be safe to drink. The maps also showed us the distances between petrol "stations" – an important factor when they could be 250 miles or more apart. To complicate fuel calculations, the advertised petrol consumption for the 2-litre engine was approximately 20 mpg but we never got near this figure in Africa. We also had to bear in mind that not all marked petrol stations would necessarily have petrol when we reached them. Equally important, the maps showed the routes across the desert and how they were marked, whether by kilometre posts or oil drums - or not at all - and the quality of the prepared road surface, usually poor, awful, or even non-existent.

In order to carry our spare set of off-road tyres, we fitted two metal bars above the cab. We were thus able to support the tyres easily. But the bars meant that the canvas hood could no longer quite reach to the top of the windscreen because it was stretched over the bars and now left a gap between the end of the canvas and the windscreen of about an inch. The hood was also no longer stretched as tightly as it had been. When it rained, a pool of water formed in the slight dip of the canvas and the water overflowed into the cab whenever we braked or changed down a gear.

There was no syncromesh gearing except between third and fourth gears, so we had to double declutch to change down below third. However the slowness of what were effectively two gear changes in the double declutch procedure meant that we soon learned we could change out of the original gear into neutral, move our legs to one side, wait a second or two for the water to pour into the cab and drain through one of the several holes in the floor and then change down into the required gear while our legs remained dry(ish). One other major difference from vehicles today was that the Land Rover did not have power steering so that, after we'd driven it for a couple of hours, we felt that we had done a considerable amount of work. That was off-road and on the roads around Birmingham and we had no real idea of what to expect when we got to Africa – but we found out.

When we eventually began our journey, in October 1966, we had covered every eventuality – we thought. We had a compass in case we lost the desert track. If we broke the compass, we knew how to find our direction by using a watch and the sun, or even just a stick and the sun. Both these skills had been learned many years previously from the *Eagle* comic or some such essential boys' reading.

You must remember that, once we started on our real desert journey, we could be out of contact with anyone else for days – or weeks, if we lost our way – in those days there were no mobile phones which we could use to call for assistance - so our Michelin maps and our ability to work out our direction as mentioned above could be the difference between a successful adventure and dying in the Sahara.

We had read everything we could about travel in Africa, especially across the Sahara. We had had all the innoculations for travelling in Africa and we had started our course of daily anti-malaria tablets. We even had a shotgun (which cost us £12 – about £200 in 2014 values) for security, which shows how naïve we were.

En Route At Last and An Interesting Offer From Another Blonde

So, we set off from Birmingham and headed for Dover. There we filled up our tanks and jerrycans with our full capacity of fifty-two gallons of petrol to get us through France and into Andorra in the Pyrenean Mountains where we again filled up with enough cheap petrol to get to Gibraltar. In Dover, our fifty-two gallons cost us £10 (equal to £170 in 2014). It was even cheaper in Andorra. We travelled through France and Spain without incident. We did notice how the mountain ranges affected the climate. In France, north of the Pyrenees, the weather was cold and snowy and snowploughs were clearing the road into Andorra. As soon as we crossed the mountain ridge onto the Spanish side, the weather was considerably warmer but still wet. We drove southwards across Spain without incident and by the time we crossed the Sierra Nevada in southern Spain, we were enjoying warm, sunny days where the oranges were ripening on the trees by the roadside.

We stayed at a campsite in southern Spain one night and met several other people intending to cross the Sahara. Two of them from London were in an Austin Mini and they were planning to travel in it to Rhodesia (now Zimbabwe) where the minority white Government had recently declared independence from Britain. The two Londoners got stuck in the mud at the campsite, so we did not think much of their chances of reaching Rhodesia. Six weeks later, we heard that they were crossing the Sahara by loading their Mini on to the top of a trans-desert truck. We never found out if they reached their destination.

When we got to Gibraltar, we found that the Spanish had closed the border for vehicles, so we left the Land Rover safely garaged on the Spanish side and walked across the border. Gibraltar was a revelation to us. It was like stepping back into England in the 1950s or, maybe even the 1930s. There were red telephone boxes and pillar boxes, Union Jacks flying from every public building, police-men exactly like at home but all with Mediterranean complexions, full English breakfasts but everyone speaking Spanish. We stayed overnight in a B & B, took the cable car to the top of the Rock, photographed the famous Barbary apes – two of which, in grati-tude, tried to steal Carl's camera. And, we looked across the nine miles of water, which was all that now separated us from: **Africa!**

Next day, after deciding we had seen enough in Gibraltar, we were walking along the main street, Winston Churchill Avenue, back to Spain, carrying our rucksacks, when we were stopped by a very good looking blonde (again!) in her twenties. She asked us where we were from and, when we said "Birmingham", she asked us if we would like to help crew a yacht across the Atlantic to the West Indies.

Now, when I was younger I had often daydreamed about sailing the *Spanish Main* and going to such exotic places as Hispaniola, Port of Spain and Santo Domingo but the facts that we had a Land Rover waiting for us and that Birmingham was not widely known as a yachting centre made us reluctantly turn down her request – reluctantly in view of the very fine view we got as she walked away from us in her shorts.

So, back to Spain and on to Algeciras, six miles away, where we boarded the car ferry to Ceuta. The distance between Algeciras, in Spain and Ceuta, in Africa, was about 15 miles but, because Ceuta was Spanish territory and strongly garrisoned by the Spanish army, the fare was subsidised. Our inter-continental voyage cost us 27 shillings (£1 35p) for the Land Rover and 5 shillings (25p) third class for each of us. As we spent the voyage on deck looking at the African coast or in the bar, and as there was only one bar for all classes, we were quite happy with third class travel.

And now, the moment we'd waited for - our adventure was about to begin in earnest! We did not stay in Ceuta but headed for the border with Morocco as soon as we disembarked. Oddly enough, for someone who when I was about ten, had fantasised about being a smuggler with a fast speedboat in the Mediterranean, we did not go to Tangiers, the nearest city in Morocco which had until ten years previously been an international Free City, famous for smuggling, dodgy expatriates and spies (think of the film *Casablanca* for the general idea). Instead, we headed directly for the Atlantic coast and the capital, Rabat. There, we were driving along one of the main roads when we noticed we were being followed by an old Citroen 2CV with its lights flashing and the driver hanging out of the window, waving his arm.

Thinking that something must have fallen off the Land Rover, we pulled in and waited for the 2CV to catch up, only to find that the driver, who was a Scottish vet working in Rabat, had noticed the British registration plate and simply wanted to talk to someone in English! We stayed with the vet for the rest of the day and he took us to a local restaurant for dinner. The drive to the restaurant was unusual, mainly because the Citroen's front seats had an aluminium frame with a piece of canvas slung from it, very much like a garden chair. This system meant that, when you went round a corner, the canvas swung on the frame and you stayed upright but the rest of the car tilted to one side, giving you a very strange feeling.

Shepherd, sheep and goats - south of the Atlas Mountains, Morocco

The following day, the vet checked up at the Foreign Ministry whether the border between Morocco and Algeria was open, as the previous year there had been a border war between the two countries. Assured that the border was open, we set off towards the frontier in the southeast, having switched our road tyres for the cross country ones.

We left Rabat and headed southeastwards, climbing up into the Atlas Mountains. As we climbed up into the cool mountain air, we began to appreciate why so many Moroccans wore long, thick woollen *djellabas* with hoods, like the dressing gowns boxers wear into the ring before a fight.

In the Moroccan countryside, we saw young boys herding sheep and goats. It was often difficult to tell these animals apart because the sheep were not woolly, as we were used to seeing, but hairy. In fact the only differences I could see were that the sheep's tails hung down, while the goats' short tails stuck up and that the goats were much more adventurous than the sheep. One particularly enterprising goat was standing on the roof of a battered car in order to reach some especially juicy leaves growing high up on an old tree. Seeing a flock of sheep or goats made the scene quite biblical (except for the car), with the shepherd walking in front and the sheep and goats following him rather than the shepherd walking behind as in England, driving the animals before him.

In the old towns we passed through, these mixed flocks were to be seen wandering along the streets. People would put out their rubbish each day in heaps against the outside wall of their houses in the dusty side streets. A flock of sheep and goats would come along and eat everything edible (including paper, as far as the goats were concerned) leaving a small amount of bottles, tin cans, etc. After this initial sorting, the much reduced rubbish pile was cleared away by the street cleaners who could salvage much of what they took away. It was a very simple but very efficient form of low-tech recycling, long before we thought of intensive recycling in Birmingham.

Driving through the passes between the mountains was like driving through high mountain regions of Europe, except that the roads were not as good. There were terraced fields, mountain flowers, stone built houses and villages with minarets pointing into the sky in place of the church spires of Europe. In both continents, the mountain air had a freshness that the air of the plains does not and the water in the mountain streams was crystal clear and icy cold but, after our camping trip in Ireland, we remembered to check upstream for rotting sheep before replenishing our water supply!

On a real road South of the Atlas Mountains, Morocco

The Land Rover heading into the desert

One night as we sat in our tent on the southern (that is, Saharan) slopes of the mountains, I remember saying that we had read as much as we could find about travelling across the Sahara and that everyone we had read about had had adventures ranging from the interesting to the dangerous. This was not going to be the case on our trip. We had already travelled 600 miles through Morocco (not to mention over 1,500 miles in Europe) and nothing out of the ordinary had happened. The next day, as we headed towards Figuig, on the border with Algeria, we were stopped by a Moroccan police patrol and warned not to go off the road at any point as some mine fields had not been cleared after the recent border war. However, eventually we were allowed to proceed and reached the border safely.

We completed the formalities at the Moroccan border post and then we drove towards the Algerian army post through a short no-mans land. Just short of the Algerian post, we came to a strong barbed wire fence. There was no gate and the fence was impassable in anything less than a tank. The information we had been given at the Foreign Ministry in Rabat was technically correct and the border crossing was open – on the Moroccan side. What nobody had thought to tell us was that the Algerians had a different idea and, as far as they were concerned, the border was most definitely closed. And all our pleading with Algerian border guards was not going to make any difference.

As we looked down the slope into Algeria, we could see the road, which would be the start of our real desert journey. It was less than a mile away. In order to reach that road we had to 250 miles northwards, on the Moroccan side of the border, to Oujda which was the only official crossing and then nearly 300 miles southwards on the Algerian side of the border.

We reached the Moroccan border post at Oujda, along the Route Nationale 17 (I shudder to think what the Routes 18, 19, etc. were like). We were hot, tired and not very well disposed to Algerian border police who had caused this detour. However, we got through the border easily enough this time. Reaching the customs post at Maghnia, about four miles inside Algeria, we had to fill in the required forms and answer the required questions. Then we had to unload the Land Rover so it could be searched. Although we had covered it up, we had not tried to hide our shotgun, so it was soon discovered.

We were told that we could only bring the gun into Algeria if we had an official permit and that, in order to get the permit we would have to go the provincial capital, about twenty-five miles away. By this time, we were fed up with driving up and down the border and we told the police officer that the shotgun was only intended for small birds. In fact, it was our idea of self-protection and the ammunition was the biggest size you could legally get for a shotgun, apart from single ball cartridges. The officer pretended to believe us and allowed us to bring the gun into Algeria. However, he did not give us any import document and that soon caused us a problem, which I will explain later.

Geographically, there was not a great deal of difference between the semi- desert areas south of the Atlas Mountains in Morocco and the semi-desert in northern Algeria. However, there was an immediate difference between the two countries in the posters displayed on the walls of buildings. In Morocco, these were usually advertisements for *Orangina*, *Coca Cola* or some similar soft drink. In Algeria most of the posters were political, urging people to support the new revolutionary Government that had taken power a few months previously in a coup. Whereas the posters in Morocco were colourful, those in Algeria were mostly drab and khaki coloured, not much different from the colour of the surrounding countryside. This difference was also reflected in the attitude of the police in the two countries.

A Good Turn For Yet Another Blonde, "Gun Running", Bobbee Moore - and Wanted By Interpol

The Sahara Desert covers almost one-third of Africa and effectively stretches from the Atlantic Ocean to the Red Sea and from the shores of the Mediterranean as far south as Nigeria. While everywhere is very dry, most of it is not covered by the sand dunes which we see in Hollywood films although these do exist over wide areas, especially in the *Great Eastern Erg* (Sea of Sand) and the *Great Western Erg*. Most of the desert surface is made up of flat, rocky plains, called *"Regs"*, flat sandy or dusty plains with scattered rocks and mountain areas. Our route across the Sahara was to take us along the edges of the Great Western Erg, through the plateaus and mountains of central Algeria and then through the lower-lying sandy and rocky plains stretching into Niger, the country between Algeria and Nigeria.

Apart from the vastness of the desert, the constant dust and sand, which got everywhere, even into the food and the flies, which also got everywhere, even into the food, one of the first things we noticed about the Sahara was the sky at night. Because of the clearness of the night air, there were so many stars that I found it impossible to recognise a single constellation.

We were in the Sahara for much of November and December and this is a time when several meteor showers take place. These reach their peak about mid-November. The year we were in the Sahara (1966) saw one of the most spectacular displays on record, with more than a thousand meteors an hour shooting across the night sky at times. On more than one occasion, we lay outside our tent gazing at the sky for two or three hours, unable to go to sleep because we had never seen anything like the magnificent light display above us. I think it was after one of these star gazing sessions that Carl announced he intended get the real experience of the desert and take a detour of over one thousand miles to Tombouctou (Timbuktu) by *camel!* - a journey which would take nearly two months. There we would rendezvous and both of us continue our journey in the Land Rover. It took me the best part of two days to convince him that such a venture was not only impracticable but also impossible.

We took a few days to adjust to driving in the desert, often away from anything resembling a road or, even a track. Our first problem, but not a major one, was getting stuck, not in sand, but in thick clay. We had to use our spade and the sand ladders to get the Land Rover out. We placed the sand ladders under the wheels to give a surface, which the tyres could grip and slowly tried to reverse out. This sounds a lot easier than it actually was but, after what seemed like an hour, we managed to get the Land Rover back on firm ground. We measured the rut we had created – it was almost thirty yards long. This was the first of many times we had to use the sand ladders.

It wasn't long before we came upon one of the huge trans-desert trucks that travelled regularly across the desert. It was the first of many we saw which had got stuck in soft sand. When one of these trucks got stuck like this, the only solution was to wait overnight when the temperature fell, sometimes to near freezing and or even below. By dawn, the sand would be cold to the touch and the grains would have become packed together, giving a firmer surface than during the day. The sand ladders could now be used and the truck manoeuvred out of danger. It was so cold in this area that when we opened a tin of Tate & Lyle syrup, the contents had solidified and we couldn't spread our bread until almost noon. On the other hand, even in November the daytime temperature rose high enough for us to fry eggs on the bonnet of the Land Rover.

Trans-Saharan truck with sand ladder strapped to the side

After a couple of days of fairly difficult but more or less uneventful driving and a sandstorm that kept us confined to our tent for a day and a half, we decided to treat ourselves and stay the night at a comfortable desert hotel in the town of Béni Abbès. The hotel even had a proper restaurant. This would, we felt, be our last night of comfort before getting to the *real* Sahara of our youthful dreams (fuelled by tales of Beau Geste and Luck of the Legion). For a touch of luxury, we decided to treat ourselves to some exotic French cuisine and ordered *cervelles* for dinner. As we were waiting for our meal, I was trying to remember what the word *"cervelles"* meant. Just as the waiter emerged from the kitchen with our dinner, I remembered that *"cerveau"* meant *"brain"* and, therefore *"cervelles"* meant *"little brains"*. There was absolutely no way I was going to eat brains. Carl, however, was more adventurous in the matter of food than I was and he waited with interest for the plates to arrive. When they did, he was ready to tuck in until we both smelled the rotten aroma rising from our dinner. Even Carl's cast-iron appetite was unable to tackle this particular exotic French/Algerian cuisine and we ended up being rather less adventurous with an omelette.

At breakfast the next morning, we were approached by a young blonde woman of about 28 (I *really* didn't have a thing about blondes!) who asked if we were going across the desert. When we said we were, she asked if we could give a lift to her and her husband who was a writer. She explained that they had planned to cross the Sahara by the regular trans-Saharan bus service. What they had just learned was that the bus service had ended two or three years previously, shortly after the French withdrew from Algeria after independence

Of course, we could not leave them stranded, even if it was through their own stupidity, and agreed to take them with us. Things went on smoothly enough for the first two days, although the husband was moody and not very communicative. Then we stopped in Adrar at another desert "hotel", this one not nearly as comfortable as the previous one. Carl got up about half past six to do some minor repairs on the Land Rover, while I had a lie-in.

After about half an hour, he came back to the bedroom and said: *"We've got a problem."*

My first thought was that he'd discovered something seriously wrong with the engine but he explained the problem was worse than that.

It turned out that the 28-year-old "wife" was actually 19 and she was not married. She had been living in Paris with her parents. Her father was an American navy captain, attached to NATO headquarters there. She had seen an advertisement from her companion, who was a 35-year-old Scottish travel writer, living in the South of

France, seeking a secretary to accompany him on a six-month journey in Africa. She had applied for the job, he had met her and her parents in Paris and they had given her permission to go with him (in those days the age of majority was twenty-one, so she had to get their permission). Why they had done this was something we could not understand, although the writer was a very plausible character and could be very charming when he wanted to be.

Anyway the girl, whose name was Shelley, was crying in the Land Rover and was not going to go any further with "that man". After talking to both and confirming that they had fallen out completely with each other, we took the writer to the local airstrip from where he flew to Algiers and then on to Paris, threatening all sorts of dire consequences for us. He cabled Shelley's parents and told them that their daughter had gone off with two penniless vagabonds. This annoyed us considerably - not the "vagabonds" bit because that sounded romantic and adventurous - but we were certainly not penniless.

We also later discovered that her father, probably because of his official position with the US NATO delegation, had enough influence to get us put on Interpol's wanted for questioning list. Interpol never found us.

Shelley continued on with us.

Two or three days later, we drove into Reggane, a small, dusty town near which the French had tested nuclear bombs in the atmosphere up to five years previously. As we stopped in the main square, we were approached by two policemen. To this day, I am convinced that the reason for what followed was the fact that we were the first travellers to stop in the town for days and the policemen just wanted something to do to relieve the boredom. After chatting for a while, they decided to search the Land Rover and watched while we unloaded everything. Very soon they came across our shotgun.

"Où est votre permis d'importation?" (*"Where is your import permit?"*)

"Nous n'en avons pas".(*"We don't have one."*)

"Pourquoi?" (*"Why not?"*)

"Because the border official in Maghnia who let us bring it into Algeria didn't give us one."

"This is very irregular. You'll have to see the Captain. Come into the police station."

Of course the Captain was not in the police station, so we had to wait. Eventually, he arrived after about two hours. He was large and not at all friendly looking.

"It is a very serious offence to smuggle guns into the country - a very serious offence. Only six weeks ago, we arrested a German trying to smuggle guns to the rebels"

He did not explain how the rebel's stocks of weapons would be much improved by one single-bore Spanish shotgun which had cost us £12. He pulled out a sheet of paper and started to write a report number on it.

"Passeports!"

We handed over one British, one Irish and one American passport. At that time both British and Irish passports were very impressive, hard-covered documents The Captain picked up the British passport and looked through it as if he was expecting to find another gun in it.

"Angleterre?" *"What is the name of your village?"*

Carl and I looked at each other.

"Birmingham", we answered.

"Ber-meeng-am? Ber-meeng-am? I have a cousin in Ber-meeng-am. Do you know him?"

"I think we may have met him once."

After that, the atmosphere of suspicion changed completely and we were soon chatting about Manchester United, Liverpool, Bobbee Moore, who had captained the victorious England World Cup team a few months previously, and Queen *Lizbet* and drinking bottles of lukewarm *Orangina*.

Reggane was not the sort of place you wanted to stay too long in so, after re-packing the Land Rover, we shook hands with the Captain and the two policemen who had started all this, and went on our way towards In Salah, 150 miles to the east, one of the hottest and driest places on earth. We didn't linger in In Salah either and headed southeast towards the mountain region of the Hoggar Massif.

The Hoggar Mountains cover a large part of southern Algeria and the peaks rise to over 9,000 feet above sea level while the average height is over 3,000 feet. There is virtually no rain but a few *wadis* (dried up beds of ancient rivers which survive as seasonal underground rivers) have stretches of drought-resistant bushes. In fact, in many places in the Sahara and other deserts there are straggly lines of thorny trees and bushes which follow the course of these underground relics of wetter times, sometimes for dozens of miles.

With The Foreign Legion

The desert surface, which had been more or less flat and dusty, rather than sandy, became more rocky as we gradually climbed into the mountains and it was now necessary to stay on the trails which were full of bumps and potholes. We had stopped near a disused fort called In Eker about 4 o'clock one afternoon to check the suspension. We soon discovered that one of the rear shock absorbers was broken. As we stood looking at this and wondering should we replace the damaged shock there and then, or should we set up camp for the night and do the repair next day in the cooler morning air, we were amazed to see six French Foreign *légionaires* appear from a side valley.

They explained that they were based at one of a number of camps nearby. When we told them what had happened, four of them went to inspect the suspension but two asked if they could take a look at the engine. Of course, we had no problem with this but we did have a problem a couple of minutes later when one of them called us over and showed us a crack in one of the two long main box beams of the chassis. In fact, it had cracked on three sides and was held together only by the metal of the top surface of the box. It also became clear that one of the rear springs needed to be replaced, too.

One of the légionaires pointed out that we wouldn't get another hundred kilometres (sixty miles) with the chassis in that condition and said we should come into their camp while they arranged the repair. So, we carefully drove the short distance into the Foreign Legion camp. This was actually a sub-camp, one of several surrounding the main base. Although Algeria had become independent from France in 1962, large numbers of French troops remained to protect the nuclear testing sites. The last, underground, nuclear bomb test had taken place nine months previously, in the area where we now found ourselves and the Foreign Legion troops were engaged in securing equipment and collecting it into the main camp for transport back to France.

We were made very welcome at the sub-camp and enjoyed an excellent dinner, which was immeasurably better than the ones we had been eating up to now. This was not surprising since the food and wine were flown in twice a week from France. There were about twenty Legionaires and they were delighted to have us as their guests. Actually, that's not quite true. They were delighted to have a young woman as their guest and they behaved with perfect manners and gallantry towards her and with polite tolerance towards Carl and myself. We managed to hold a pleasant conversation conducted in a mixture of English and French.

At the dinner table, I was sitting opposite one soldier who did not join in the conversation but who drank considerably more wine than anyone else. He kept staring at Shelley and the look on his face as he stared at her was less than pleasant. I remember thinking that I hoped we would not have any trouble because we would be honour bound to protect Shelley but what could two of us do against twenty Foreign Legion soldiers? Our shotgun would be useless and might lead to us being injured or shot and, anyway, it was in the Land Rover. That thought showed how little I knew about the Foreign Legion in spite of being a keen reader of *Luck of the Legion* in the *Eagle* comic in my youth. The rest of the soldiers didn't seem to notice anything amiss and continued as pleasantly as before.

After dinner, we were shown into an unused storeroom to make ourselves as comfortable as possible for the night on the camp beds with which we had got out of the Land Rover. We took the precaution of locking the door and, about half an hour later, there was a knock and the sound of someone turning the handle. Immediately, we were alert and asked;

"Qui est là? Que voulez-vous?" *(Who's there? What do you want?")*

"Je veux parler." *("I want to talk".)* It was the soldier who had been opposite me at dinner.

"Non. Allez-vous en!" *("No. Go away!")*

He moved away and then tried to get open the wooden shutter which covered the window (there wasn't any glass). He was so drunk that I managed to force the shutter closed again even though he was obviously much stronger and fitter than I was. Then he forced open the shutter again and threw a knife through. This hit me but fortunately his aim was so bad that it was the handle and not the blade that hit me.

By this time we were shouting for help and, very soon we heard someone running along the corridor. Obviously our would-be visitor heard the footsteps too, for he disappeared.

"Qu'est-ce qui se passe?" (What's going on?) It was the voice of the corporal in charge.

We opened the door and explained what had happened. The corporal, who was armed with a sub-machine gun and carried a torch, was incandescent with rage. The drunken soldier had violated the basic principles of hospitality and would obviously have violated much more if he had got away with it.

It only took a minute to find the soldier in the next storeroom. The corporal gave me the torch and went in and beat the soldier up without mercy. He punched him, kicked him and, when he was lying on the floor, kicked him again in the ribs. Then the corporal picked up a heavy wooden ammunition box and raised it above his head. I thought

"If this hits the soldier on the head, it'll kill him!"

However, the corporal threw it down on his chest. Then he went out into the corridor, picked up the machine gun and loaded it:

"Please, God, don't let him kill him!

Then he took out the magazine, had second thoughts, loaded it again, gave the gun to me and said,

"If he moves, shoot him!"

I had one hand on the butt and the other on the barrel and kept the gun carefully pointed up at the ceiling, while the corporal went out into the corridor to cool down.

"I fought in the Second World War," said the corporal when he came back, *"I fought in Indo-China, I have slit men's throats. But this, this is intolerable!"*

You see, we had been invited into the camp; we were the guests of the Legion and under its protection. The soldier had committed the worst crime possible – he had dishonoured the Legion.

The soldier was sitting up by this time and the corporal made him come on his knees into the room where we had left Shelley and apologise to her and then to Carl and myself. He asked us to sign a paper stating that he (the corporal) had been attacked by the soldier. We signed. The truth was that all the time the corporal had been punching and kicking him, the soldier had made no attempt to defend himself but had taken all the damage the corporal had inflicted on him without any response. By now, other légionaires had arrived and the corporal ordered two of them to escort the soldier to one of the other sub-camps.

If the légionaires had been kind and hospitable to us up to this point, nothing was too much trouble for them from now on. It was as if they were trying to wipe out what they perceived as a stain on the Legion's honour.

The next day, the corporal asked Carl and me if we wanted to go and see our intruder in the other sub-camp. We weren't very keen but felt that we couldn't refuse. So we went off in a jeep and there was the soldier, battered and bruised, half lying on a bunk bed, reading. But the most impressive fact was that, if it was necessary, he was ready for action. I realised then just how tough the men of the Foreign Legion were and that I was very glad that the rest of them were on our side.

While we were at this second sub-camp we noticed a small mountain range in the middle distance and also noticed that there was dust coming from a cave or vent in the side of one of the mountains. This dust rose up into the sky and then started to form a mushroom shape. The mountain range was between us and the site of France's underground nuclear bomb tests, the last of which, as I have already mentioned, was supposed to have taken place nine months previously.

We did not hear any sound, or feel any tremors but, as we watched the cloud become more and more mushroom shaped, a jeep came from the direction of the main camp and the corporal went to talk to its occupants. Then the jeep roared off in the direction of the mountains and the corporal returned to where we were waiting. We asked him what the cloud meant, only to be told that it was nothing important. We never did get any explanation of this strange occurrence.

Back at the sub-camp arrangements had been made for us to get the Land Rover repaired. However, it was decided that the fewer people who knew about Shelley, the better. So we were taken to the main camp after dark and smuggled into the sergeants' mess. If the food at the sub-camp was good, at the main camp it was even better. Again, our Legion helpers were more than helpful and we set off late the next day, fully checked and repaired and with petrol, water and food supplies restored. It was only about 150 miles to Tamanrasset, the main town in Southern Algeria and the track (Route Nationale 1), while it was a National Road in name only, was no worse than anything we had already experienced.

You're Not Going To Believe This!

When we reached Tamanrasset, we had to report to the police for permission to cross the next part of the Sahara, as far as the border with Niger. Unless you were driving a cross-country vehicle, as we were, you had to wait in Tamanrasset to make up a convoy with at least two of these vehicles. Already waiting was another Land Rover and about six Volkswagen Camper vans and Bedford Dormobiles. So, as we provided the second Land Rover, the convoy got permission to proceed.

Tamanrasset, itself, was a sizeable town built around an oasis where dates, figs, corn and oranges are grown. Most of the inhabitants were Tuareg who regarded themselves as kings of the desert and superior to the Arab officials and troops who represented the Government here. Camels roamed through the sandy streets, ready for their owners to load them up with sticks, paraffin, fruit, bags of corn, sugar, cloth, salt and countless other goods for transport goodness knows how many miles across the desert, along tracks that no vehicle could follow.

Everywhere in the Sahara can be dangerous and the desert south of Tamanrasset was particularly so. Only about two months before we were setting off to the south, a German couple and their twenty year old daughter had lost their way about sixty miles from Tamanrasset. When they were found – dead – about three weeks later, they were only a mile from the track.

Camels loaded up in Tamanrasset

They had made a number of fundamental mistakes. One, they were travelling alone, two, they had told no one of their route, intended destination or estimated arrival time and three, when they broke down, they tried to walk to safety without knowing how far away that safety was.

Meet the Neighbours

To try and prevent this sort of thing happening, the French had regulated all travel south of Tamanrasset so that everyone travelled in convoys and each convoy had to give an estimate of their arrival at the next major stopping point. The idea was that, if you failed to appear at the next stop by a day or two after the expected time, a search party could be sent out with a good chance of rescuing you.

This system worked well most of the time when the French still controlled the country but after independence, the Algerians had changed it slightly although they still kept the convoys. Experienced travellers alleged that the new system was that authorities did not think there was much wrong until you were at least a week overdue and, by that time you'd be dead anyway, so there was no point in sending out a search party.

So, our convoy set off from Tamanrasset. In our Land Rover we carried our full complement of fifty-two gallons of petrol and twenty gallons of water. We didn't realise that our water supply was more than adequate for two people but not three by the official recommendations. However, as it turned out, we did not have any water problems. One Land Rover took the lead, followed by the Volkswagens and Dormobiles, and then the second Land Rover took up the rear. The lead Land Rover would drive ahead for ten minutes, or so, then stop. If we could see a cloud of dust behind, we would carry on for another ten minutes. If there was no dust, it meant someone had got stuck, so we had to go back and pull it, or them out. This would happen six or seven times a day. Without the Land Rovers, the other vehicles wouldn't have travelled more than a dozen miles a day, if they had even been able to get that far. Of course, the tracks have *(probably)* greatly improved since 1966.

The track between Tamanrasset and In Guezzam on the border with Niger was particularly difficult. We drove through a pass between mountains and had seas of sand all around. The Volkswagens and Dormobiles kept getting stuck and even the Land Rovers had difficulty getting through and pulling the other vehicles out. Our sand ladders were working overtime.

In Guezzam consisted of a few ramshackle buildings and a well and, maybe a mile or so away, the official border post. The well had a square of tin covering it and the water lay about eight feet below the sand and had to be hauled up in a jerrycan with a suspiciously fraying rope attached to the handle. It was the first water since Tamanrasset (a distance of over 250 miles) and the only available for another 130 miles, so we replenished our supplies of both water and petrol, the latter from 250 litre (55 gallon) drums by a wayside shack. It didn't inspire us with the greatest confidence about the quality of the petrol when we saw small twigs disappearing into our petrol tanks. However, the Land Rover coped with the less than ideal octane level. We had our passports stamped as we exited Algeria and moved on across the border into Niger.

There was no similar border control on the Niger side and we drove for several miles into the country before we came to a police post. We stopped and reported there. Only about four of the fifteen or so people in our convoy had visas for Niger but that was not a problem and the rest of us were all issued with visas and vehicle import documents. The whole process was conducted with admirable efficiency within a couple of hours, including the collection of visa charges which, oddly enough, varied according to nationality.

Once we had completed all the formalities, we did not linger at the post but pressed on; following a track that was only shown by markers set a kilometre apart (in theory). The track itself was very rutted in many places, so it was easier to drive on the open desert surface which was quite hard and where we could sometimes reach speeds of up to fifty mph. The rest of the day went off without any new problems and we only needed to rescue the other vehicles a few times.

The next day started off in much of the same way with our Land Rover going ahead of the rest of the convoy. After about two hours, I took over the driving from Carl. After a further two hours of relatively easy driving, we came to a point where the hard open desert surface was blocked by a wide rocky outcrop and it was necessary to drive for about a mile on the badly rutted track. Our speed dropped down to a very bumpy less than ten mph and I could not avoid a series of deep potholes. I was surprised when one hole proved especially hard to get out off. I changed down to the lowest of our eight forward gears but still could not make any progress. I looked out off the side window and actually said:

"You're not going to believe this!"

"What?"

"Look over there."

"Over there" was about three feet away from the Land Rover, where the rear wheel was lying on the ground. That in itself was not a great problem because we were well capable of dealing with such a situation. What was going to be a problem was that the wheel has still attached to the axle, half of which was also three feet away from the Land Rover and pointing vertically up to the sky.

Now, we had brought tools and spare parts to cover all conceivable accidents and potential problems, *except* having a half shaft decide to go walkabout and part company with the rest of the Land Rover.

As we got out and stood, scratching our heads and looking at the unusual sight which faced us, this time we did not have a group of Foreign Legion soldiers arrive to help us. However, we only had to wait for about twenty minutes before the rest of the convoy caught up with us and stood scratching their heads, too.

It seems we have a problem!

Since we were blocking the track, the other Land Rover pulled us along to a flat space where the other vehicles could pass us and then we all got out and scratched our heads again. The rocky area had trapped some of the scanty rainfall (we were near the southern edge of the desert) and, although there wasn't any surface water, there was some sparse grass and a few thorny trees.

We soon decided that the only thing to do was for Carl to go on with the rest of the convoy to the nearest town, Agadès, over 140 miles away, and seek help, while I stayed with the Land Rover to make sure it was safe until he returned. I wasn't particularly happy about being on my own, in the desert but I was very surprised when Shelley said she would stay with me. Whatever about a man being on his own in the Sahara, I wasn't at all sure that it was wise for a young woman to stay. However, she did and we settled down to wait for Carl's return with help in a couple of days. We had our tent, enough water for five days, plenty of food and the famous shotgun.

Although I was glad to have Shelley's company, I had doubts about how effective the shotgun would be as a defence and I was a bit worried about being able to protect her (and myself) if the need arose. Only twenty minutes after Carl and the others had left us, my worries on this score increased when we had a visitor. When I look back on the incident, he was probably a goat herder but his sudden appearance immediately made me think where there was one person who could maybe take a fancy to Shelley, there were probably others and I looked round to make sure the shotgun and ammunition were within reach. As it happened, I need not have worried. He was not involved in the white slave traffic and the scene turned into a sort of Saharan *"Coronation Street"* episode because all he wanted was a cup of sugar and, when he got this, he went off happily. I have the feeling that, in today's world, a similar situation would not be so simple to deal with and it might not have such an easy ending.

Carl returned the next day in a jeep with a mechanic and a spare half shaft. This was soon fixed into our Land Rover and we followed the jeep to Agadès. On the journey, Carl told us that he had only hired the half shaft at an exorbitant cost of £50 (£850 in 2014 values). When we got to the garage in Agadès, we had to return the half shaft and we found out that the nearest place we could get a new one was 700 miles away in Nigeria and we would have to wait six weeks for delivery. So, we were stuck until the garage owner came up with a satisfactory solution. Satisfactory for him, that was!

Our ten-year-old Land Rover was in excellent shape but for the fact that it was missing half an axle. The garage owner had an eighteen-year-old version, which was in poor condition, but it *was* fully supplied with axles. What could be simpler than taking a good half shaft out of his 1948 vehicle and fitting it into our well-maintained (thanks to the Foreign Legion) version? Instead of having two wrecks, there would now be one reliably usable Land Rover. Of course, before this could happen, we would have to sell him our vehicle, which was obviously of no further use to us. So, that is what we did and, as we were in no position to haggle, the price paid for our Land Rover was equivalent to only £80 (£1360 in 2014 values), less than twice what we'd paid to rent the half shaft! But then, we had zero bargaining power about the price we got. What made things even harder to bear was seeing "our" Land Rover being driven around the streets of Agadès only two hours after the sale, with the good half shaft in it so that it was in nearly as good condition as when we started out from England.

We now had all our luggage from the Land Rover and no way of getting it anywhere. So we sorted out what we needed and could carry between us and decided to sell the rest in the local market place. Spare clothes, tinned food, our shotgun; all went for whatever few francs we could get. The only thing we didn't manage to sell was our inflatable boat – there wasn't much call for it in the desert, even though we tried to re-brand it as a paddling pool or water container for animals to drink from.

Next, we negotiated a ride on a trans-Saharan truck heading for Kano in Nigeria. I'm not sure what class of travel this was but it wasn't too bad, considering that we were sitting on top of a load of dates in sacks, along with nearly thirty other people. Everyone was quite cheerful and quite a few could speak some French, so the time passed enjoyably enough except for stiff legs and sore backs. The distance to the border with Nigeria was just under 400 miles, so we did the journey in two days and arrived at the Nigerian border post about half an hour after it closed for the night on Christmas Eve, 1966.

"We Were *British* Trained"

Although the border post had closed, we were allowed to bed down in the waiting area with the luggage we had salvaged so as to be ready when the post opened the next morning (Christmas Day). Someone had left behind a copy of one of the national newspapers. The main story was headlined in huge type:

"CIVIL WAR?"

That was our welcome to Nigeria. In fact, the civil war did not break out for another six months.

The border post opened at eight o'clock on Christmas morning. We presented ourselves and our passports to the short, stout, pompous police sergeant whose attitude towards us is probably best described as that of a younger Captain Mainwaring of *"Dad's Army"*. At first, everything seemed pleasant and it was not until he saw the three passports – one British, one Irish and one American – that matters started going down hill.

Carl and I did not need a visa to enter Nigeria but, as an American, Shelley did - and she didn't have one. But, the sergeant assured us, it was not a big problem because all she had to do before she crossed the border was to go to the Nigerian embassy in Niamey, the capital of Niger, get a Nigerian visa and she would be welcome to return and enter Nigeria. Meanwhile, Carl and I could enter Nigeria and wait for her in Kano, 75 miles away. We pointed out that Niamey was almost 600 miles away, Shelley had no way of getting there and it wasn't a very good idea for a young white woman to be wandering alone around Africa. It made no difference, the sergeant insisted she could not come into Nigeria without a visa.

Then I played our trump card.

"When we crossed from Algeria into Niger with a convoy of about twelve other people, most of us didn't have visas but we reported to the first police post we came to and we all had visas in about two hours." Surely, he could do the same for this lady.

To this day, I can remember the sight of the sergeant in his khaki uniform and his reply. He pulled himself up to his full height of five foot six, puffed out his chest and, although we were taller than him, he managed to look down his nose at us as if we had something nasty on the soles of our boots:

"That may be all right for those *people! They* were French *trained. But we were* <u>British</u> *trained. You ought to know better!* He almost spat out the last sentence.

And he refused to budge from this position.

We couldn't leave Shelley to go by herself the six hundred miles to Niamey and six hundred miles back. For all three of us to go was out of the question. So, what were we to do?

The answer was actually quite simple. From where we were in the border post, we could see men and women walking across the border between the two countries without any reference to the police. Why couldn't we do the same? We knew from our map that there was another border post about twelve miles away. Why not simply walk across the border like the locals but half way between the two border posts?

So we assured the sergeant we would sort out everything in Niamey and would return to collect our luggage, which he agreed to look after for us. We walked back into Niger but then the plan fell apart. I wanted to keep walking for three miles or so, then turn east and walk at least four miles parallel to the border and only then turn south and cross the border at a point where we would not be seen. My two companions did not see any need for such exertion in the heat and dust, so we crossed the border only about a mile from where we had left the sergeant. Of course, we were seen by a number of the local people.

However, we managed to get a lift into Kano and found a hotel where we stayed for the rest of Christmas Day and Boxing Day. The expatriate community in Kano was quite small and we were immediately invited to a party where we met most of the resident Europeans, including a couple who were getting ready to leave for England as soon as they could arrange things. We were surprised at this haste because the life of an expatriate in Nigeria, in fact in any part of Africa at the time, was quite luxurious and very well paid. Someone else at the party explained the reason for the couple wanting to leave this life style so quickly.

The week before, the wife had been at Kano airport, waiting in the queue to board an internal flight. A group of half a dozen soldiers came in to the terminal and over to where she was waiting. The officer in charge asked her very politely if she would mind standing to one side. Then the officer, whose troops had surrounded the man in front of her in the queue, took out his pistol and shot the man dead. After this experience, the wife was understandably shocked and just wanted out of a country where this sort of thing could happen. Similar things were happening in an increasing number of instances during the slow but violent build up to the civil war, which was soon to be conducted with merciless brutality, particularly by the Federal Government soldiers.

The next day after ensuring Shelley was safe in the hotel, Carl and I headed back to the border. We got a lift on a lorry going into Niger and asked the driver to let us off about three miles before the border post. Our intention was to walk back across the border well away from the post and then approach it from the right direction–that is, apparently from Niger.

Unfortunately, either the driver couldn't understand our French, or he suspected we were up to no good and he drove us right up to the border post, which we therefore approached from the wrong, that is, the Nigerian, side in full view of the sergeant standing at the door. He, of course had been told about our illegal border crossing and he was not at all impressed with Carl and myself. In fact, he now looked at us not as if we had something nasty on our boots but as if we *were* that something nasty.

In spite of our insistent claim that we had arranged for Shelley to travel to Niamey and we had returned to the border post to collect the rest of our luggage and wait for her in Kano, it did not take a Sherlock Holmes to work out that we were lying. Although the sergeant was no Sherlock Holmes, he was able to give a good account of our movements since he had last seen us and of what we had done with Shelley. The only thing he didn't know was where in Kano she was waiting.

He gave this very clear account to the police chief in Kano after he escorted us there to police headquarters in the back of a commandeered Citroën van. Although the two policemen were speaking in Hausa, the main language of Northern Nigeria, their conversation was sprinkled with several references in English to unpleasant concepts, such as *"most irregular behaviour"*, *"highly suspicious"*, *"totally reprehensible and unacceptable"* and other similar expressions which did nothing to raise our rapidly sinking spirits. Eventually, the police chief told us with complete accuracy exactly what we had done and, more to the point, exactly what we were going to do - that was, leave the country immediately.

When we protested that we couldn't do that because Shelley would be coming to Kano, expecting to see us and that we would have her possessions, the police chief answered us in very clear words:

"Let me put it like this, "Gentlemen", you can either leave the country or you can go to jail."

We opted to leave the country.

This involved another 75-mile journey in the back of the Citroën van to the border post where we still had our luggage. When we arrived there, we pleaded with the sergeant to let us stay in Nigeria and eventually, after we had offered to hand over our passports to him, he agreed to let us stay on condition that we sorted out Shelley's position as soon as possible with the American embassy in Lagos. We collected our luggage and got another lift to Kano, so completing a total journey that day of 300 miles and not one of them comfortable.

By this point I was only too glad to hand over the responsibility for Shelley to the US embassy and Carl agreed this was the only solution, even though he had by now taken a fancy to her.

The Kano To Lagos Express

There was a train leaving Kano the next morning for the capital, Lagos, 700 miles away. We decided we would be on it. We arrived at Kano station about half an hour before departure, intending to buy three third class single tickets. When we got on to the platform, it was nearly impossible to even see the third class carriages. They were completely crammed with people and luggage and still people were trying to push their way on. The more athletic were climbing in through the windows. Passengers were standing on running boards and even the carriage roofs had passengers and luggage perched precariously on top. It took us about ten seconds to decide that we would not attempt third class travel.

Second class travel was considerably more expensive but the conditions were much better. Nearly everyone had a seat on a bench, maybe not comfortable but your own space, nevertheless. Departure time came..... and went but the train didn't. When it did eventually start, it was at a stately pace, which did not dislodge the passengers on the roof.

The entire journey was scheduled to take just over 24 hours. In fact it took 42, at an average speed of just under 17 miles per hour. This particular service was regularly held up by bandits and, for this reason, there was an armed police guard on the train. And when I write "an armed police guard", I mean exactly that – a *single* policeman, armed with a *single* rifle. We couldn't understand what one policeman could do to protect the passengers if there was a hold up. Maybe the policeman had the same thought and that explained what he did next – got blind drunk so that he had to be disarmed by a group of soldiers going home on leave.

We found our fellow passengers to be as interested in us as we were in them although some of them had the primary interest in persuading us that we should become Muslims, Northern Nigeria being a mostly Muslim region. After several hours, an inspector came round and moved the three of us into an empty first class compartment. This was still not luxurious except in the fact that we now had plenty of space to stretch out.

After about twelve hours into our journey, the water supply on the train ran out and we had to rely on rapidly diminishing supplies of warm beer and on drinks bought from sellers of food and soft drinks who crowded round the windows at every station when we stopped. The train continued on its stately progress and the countryside gradually changed from the dry, dusty semi-desert at the start to the open grasslands and scattered trees of the savanna and then gradually to the more intensively cultivated fields and clearings in the tropical forests as we moved south and approached Lagos, which was then the capital.

Village in Southern Nigeria as seen from the Kano – Lagos express

The people on the train also changed as we moved south. In northern Nigeria, our travelling companions were mostly from the Hausa ethnic group who wore long flowing robes but, as we travelled through central and southern Nigeria, more and more men wearing western style clothes boarded the train. And more women appeared, travelling alone or in groups, and usually loaded with various goods they intended to sell at the many markets. It was also noticeable that in the north, if someone came into our compartment, once they saw us they tended to apologise and go out again. Perhaps this was because we had Shelley with us. The further south we went, the more likely that people would enter the compartment and engage us in conversation.

One of the women who engaged us in conversation gave us a plantain as she was getting off the train. A plantain is like a very large banana and, since we were quite hungry we started to eat it. What we did not know was that, although it might look like a giant banana, a plantain needs to be cooked before eating and it was not long before the other passengers in our compartment had tears running down their faces as they laughed at our efforts to eat something as indigestible as a raw plantain. However, they were very kind and gave us various fruits and food which did not need cooking.

We arrived at the station in Lagos 42 hours after we had left Kano. The first thing we did as soon as the US Embassy opened was to take Shelley there and explain the situation to an American Consular official. Within a few days the irregular nature of our position was sorted out. Shelley stayed with the family of an Embassy official until arrangements were made to fly her back to her parents in Paris Arrangements were also made to retrieve our passports from the border police. In addition, considering the help and support we had given to an American citizen, the Embassy staff organised that all references to an illegal entry into Nigeria disappeared from official records and we were free to stay and go as we pleased. It was at this point we were told that Interpol had been looking for us.

Shelley flew to Paris a couple of days later and Carl and I were left to decide what we wanted to do next. As I mentioned before, Carl had taken a fancy to Shelley and he followed her to Paris after a further couple of days, claiming that he was only going to put the record straight with her parents. I didn't believe his explanation then and I don't believe it to this day, notwithstanding his protestations at the time and since.

I still had a fair amount of funds left, so I decided to stay for a while in Nigeria and try to get a job for long enough to raise sufficient money to continue on to South Africa, where I had an aunt who was a nun.

It didn't take long to meet various expatriates in Lagos and I was invited to lunch at the Ikoyi Club. This was like being transported back in time to the days of the Empire and many of the members had retained the old colonial attitudes towards the Nigerian staff. When it became known that I was seeking employment, I was soon offered a job in an unspecified position with Shell, which had (and still has) vast oil interests in Nigeria. I knew nothing about oil exploration or production except what any geography teacher would know but I did have all the qualifications for a junior super-visory job. In other words, I was reasonably well educated, could speak English and above all, I was *white*. That was the attitude among expatriates at the time and, in many places, for a long time after.

The problem arose when I said I wanted to stay in Nigeria for six months. Shell wanted me to commit to working for a year because of the way the work permit system was organised. When I declined to stay for so long, the job offer fell through.

Homeward Bound

After making a few more enquiries and, with my money now dwindling and feeling a bit lonely, I decided to call it a day and head for home. However, I didn't have enough money for the air ticket back to Birmingham, so, one morning, I presented myself at the Irish embassy (I was the one travelling on the Irish passport) and explained the situation to someone whom I took to be the Third Secretary but who turned out to be the Ambassador – a very pleasant gentleman called Kevin Rush.

Ambassador Rush explained the system to me. He would send a cable to the Department of External Affairs in Dublin and they would make contact with my parents in Birmingham. My parents would have to deposit £100 for the air fare back to Birmingham plus more money to cover other expenses – this amounted to a lot of money for them in 1967 (the £100 air fare alone was the equivalent of £1,700 in 2014) into a nominated bank and, once the Department had been notified of the deposit, they would cable the Ambassador and authorise him to provide me with the air ticket.

All this would take a few days and, meanwhile, I should report to the embassy each day. As I was getting up to leave, the Ambassador asked me if I was all right for money and I assured him that I was. In spite of my reply, he put his hand into his pocket and said "You'd better have this, just in case" and handed me a £10 Nigerian note. This was equivalent to £170 sterling now and over half my week's wage as a teacher back in Birmingham at the time and here was the Ambassador handing over a large sum of money like this to someone who had literally walked in off the street about forty minutes previously.

The next day, when I reported to the embassy, the Ambassador asked me if I was doing anything that evening. Since my days consisted of wandering about from one bookshop with a fan to the next with a fan or, occasionally, the heaven of air conditioning, I was able to reply with confidence that I wasn't doing anything special in the evening.

"I have to give a dinner to an important businessman. Would you like to come along?"

Of course I jumped at the chance of a decent meal – the first one since our stay with the Foreign Legion – and that is how I found myself, in the cleanest clothes I could manage, enjoying dinner in the Ikoyi Palace Hotel, at that time the top hotel in Nigeria, at the Irish taxpayers' expense with funds provided by the Department of External (now Foreign) Affairs. In case any Foreign Affairs official is worried, the dinner was excellent and I have to tell him and the Irish taxpayers that I was very grateful for their unexpected and unwitting generosity.

As the Ambassador explained, the embassy in Lagos was small and so were the numbers of Irish citizens there, so he was able to do things that would not have been possible in bigger embassies in places like London, Paris or Washington.

For the next few days, I reported to the embassy each morning about ten o'clock but no cable arrived. On the fourth or fifth day, I arrived at the embassy just after ten and still there was no news from Dublin. As I went to leave, a cable started to come through at ten minutes past ten. It said that the required money had been deposited and the embassy was authorised to issue me with an airline ticket to Birmingham.

Now things moved very fast. Mr Rush told me to collect my ticket from a certain travel agency immediately and told me there was a Swissair flight leaving for Geneva at ten to eleven, with a connecting flight to Birmingham. While he did not actually use the words, *"Be on that flight"*, his expectations were unmistakable.

I took a taxi to collect my ticket, which was already waiting for me and then rushed to the "hotel" where I was staying to pay my bill and collect my belongings before rushing to the airport. Unfortunately, in the rush I forgot my Olympus Pen half-frame camera that had all my photographs of our trans-Saharan adventure so those illustrating our adventure are ones that Carl had saved.

When the taxi arrived at the airport terminal (late), three officials were waiting outside,

"Mr Rice?" one of them asked and when I said, *"Yes"*, he grabbed me, the second official grabbed my rucksack and the third my passport. I was rushed through the terminal and as I reached the airside door, things briefly turned into something like a Hollywood spy film. The aeroplane was 200 yards away, engines revving up, first class gangway in place. A car roared up to the terminal door and stopped with brakes screeching, I was bundled in and we roared off at high speed to the aircraft steps. I'm sure the passengers who had been kept waiting by a telephone call from the embassy thought that a Government Minister or other VIP was arriving, only to see me coming up the steps with my scruffy bush jacket and rucksack and walking through the first class cabin into the economy section. The plane, at that time the fastest commercial jet, a French Caravelle, was rolling along the runway less than a minute after my sudden and belated arrival.

As I sat in my window seat on this, my first flight, I could see the wings flexing as the plane gathered speed along the tarmac. This worried me for a few moments because I had always thought of aeroplane wings as rigid, not flexible. However, no one else seemed to be worried and, after we took off and reached level flight I settled down to the six-hour journey, which passed off without incident. The only thing I now remember about the flight itself was flying between the Swiss mountains before touching down at Geneva. The sight of the snow covered Alps and the green fields on the lower slopes was amazing – like the opening scenes of *The Sound of Music.*

I arrived back in Birmingham on the last Wednesday in January 1967, about three and a half months after I had set out with high hopes to conquer Africa. As the temperature in Birmingham was just above freezing and I had been used to temperatures in Lagos of over 90°F (31°C), the first thing I did on arriving home was catch a severe cold. The second thing I did was to stay in for the next few days, feeling cold and miserable.

And that was the end of our African Adventure.

But...

What Happened Next

By the start of the following week, I had recovered enough to get myself re-employed as a teacher by Birmingham Education Committee and to feel well enough to go out with one of my friends from school to a dance at the Locarno Ballroom in the centre of Birmingham on the next Friday, nine days after arriving back.

In 1967, the Locarno Ballroom was Birmingham's leading dancehall and Friday evening was the time to go. There was a multi-coloured revolving glitterball hanging from the ceiling and a stage which also revolved to take the resident band off half way through the evening and bring on the smaller rock 'n roll group for the interval, both of them playing the same tune as the stage was turning. The dances started early, officially at eight o'clock, and were going strongly by quarter to nine. They finished before half past eleven, to allow people to catch the last daytime service bus from the city centre, before the much more expensive night time fares began, although you could stay later, if you wanted to, and dance to "records" played on a "record player". There were no such things as *"discos"* in those days.

My friend, Terry, and I arrived about quarter past eight, neatly dressed in our best clothes, with hair carefully combed and, in my case, held in place by *Trugel* (it was less obvious than Brylcreem) and shoes polished. Any possible bad breath or the smell of a small amount of "Dutch courage" from the bar were kept in check by *Amplex* tablets and Polo mints. A last minute visit to the Gents to make sure you had actually got rid of that persistent blackhead and then to find a strategic spot that gave a good view of the girls along the edge of the dance floor and of the entrance to allow us to spot the newcomers.

About half an hour after Terry and I had arrived, three girls walked in together. After taking a good look at them, I said to Terry:

"Come on, let's ask two of those girls for a dance."

The three girls, meanwhile, stood looking around. I had taken particular notice of one of them, a brunette with shoulder length nut brown hair. She was wearing a simple emerald green dress with a high neck and long sleeves, with the hem reaching just below her knees. Below the hem was a pair of very nice looking legs and the dress itself accentuated, rather than hid, her attractiveness.

I made sure I was in front of Terry as we moved towards them.

The Locarno's band, like most at the time, played sets of three dances at a time, three waltzes, then three quicksteps, three rock 'n'roll, three twists and so on, interspersed from time to time with a novelty dance like *The March of the Mods* (remember that one?). At the end of each set of three, the bandleader said:

"Thank you very much, ladies and gentlemen," and everyone moved off the dance floor to wait for the next set. The band had just started playing the second of a set of three waltzes when I made my move, like a (very nervous) trainee lion about to approach its unsuspecting prey.

"Excuse me. May I have this dance, please?"

"Yes, if you like. Thank you." (It was all very formal.)

So, on to the dance floor, with about six minutes to attempt to make some sort of good impression before the next *"Thank you very much, ladies and gentlemen."* Those six minutes were full of tension but I had to appear to be relaxed because at the end of them was the moment of truth. The most important thing I had learned during my time at College wasn't anything about teaching, or Geography, or History, my speciality subjects. It was that, if a girl danced the two or three dances of a set with you and you then asked her if she would like a drink, success or failure hung on her answer. If she agreed to have a drink, then you had the ten minutes or so taken for the drink *and* another ten minutes during the next dance set to give the impression that you weren't a complete no-hoper because most girls, if they accepted a drink from you, felt obliged to dance the next set of three dances with you.

And this was what happened. After a *snowball* (a cocktail of advocaat and lemonade, very popular as a ladies' drink at that time) the brunette, whose name was Rosemary, agreed to go back on to the dance floor with me. We danced together for the rest of the evening, even though she asked me if I wanted to dance with someone else but I insisted I didn't. She was nineteen, four years younger than I was and a nursery nurse in a local authority home for babies and young children who were not able to live with their families for one reason or another. She came across as somewhat shy but kind and caring and very attractive and, for that evening at least, I really did not want to dance with, or even to be with, anyone else.

Another thing, unlike the discos young people attend nowadays, the sound level of the music from the live band allowed you to have a conversation while you were dancing together or sitting at the side of the dance floor, even if you did have to lean close to the girl's ear – and to the rest of her – which in this case, I have to confess, was no hardship!

By the time the evening was coming to an end, I asked if I could see her the next day (Saturday). When she said *"No"*, I was taken aback because I thought we had been getting on well but she explained that she was on duty on Saturday, however she was free on Sunday, so we agreed to meet then.

Then she did what *every* girl does at dances – she disappeared into the Ladies with her friends and stayed there! I waited for five minutes for her to come out, then ten, with Terry (whom I had selfishly ignored for almost the whole of the evening) impatient to go. Then I saw her pass across the outside door to the Ladies, she looked out and saw us but carried on out of sight. This was *not* a good sign. The waiting became fifteen minutes, then twenty minutes. By this time I had come to the disappointing conclusion that Terry was right – she was not going to come out while I was waiting there.

So, Terry and I left the Locarno and walked down the street. I was definitely not happy about the way the night had finally turned out after things had seemed to be going so well.

We were less than five yards from the corner of the side street down which Terry had parked his three-wheeler Isetta bubble car.

Then came the *click, click, click* sound of high heels running along the pavement, a tug at the sleeve of my coat and, as I turned round,

"Well, <u>are</u> we seeing each other on Sunday, or aren't we?"

And that was the start of another Adventure, even bigger than Africa, which is still going on as I type these words, more than forty-seven years afterwards.

No longer a teenager, the girl with shoulder length nut brown hair, on her 22nd birthday.

and...

what she did a month later with the fella she caught up with after the dance ...

And that is *all* you're going to know!

Except...

that

    it

        was

            nowhere

                near

                    The End

Afterthoughts

The reason for the long delay in the Ladies at the Locarno was that one of Rosemary's friends had lost her handbag - at least, that was what I was told.

As it happened, the number one record in the Top Twenty that Friday was *"I'm a Believer"* by the Monkees and number 20 was *"Single Girl"* by Sandy Posey. If you can't remember the words, look up *'Youtube + the Monkees + I'm a Believer'* and *'Youtube + Sandy Posey + Single Girl'*. Even if some would say nowadays that the second one was un-feminist (I prefer to think of it as romantic), it was a strange coincidence that these particular two songs, with their respective (and, in the circumstances, highly appropriate) lyrics, should be at the two ends of the Top Twenty on the evening in 1967 I met the girl who has been my wife since 1969.

Carl's Adventures in Canada

Carl left teaching in 1970 and went to Canada. He worked at various outdoor jobs for a couple of years in Newfoundland on the Atlantic coast and every summer he would take off by himself for two or three months into the Canadian wilderness with only a tent and camping gear and a rifle to fulfil his ambition to be a backwoodsman. Sometimes, he wouldn't see another human being for a month or more. However, he did see plenty of wildlife. Some of this wildlife, he would shoot for food but he soon found that bears and other animals wanted to share in his larder. To protect his food from bears, he discovered that he had to tie a rope about fifteen, or even more, feet up between two trees about twenty feet apart. He then had to cut down any interconnecting branches and the tie his meat on a line hanging midway along the rope so that it was impossible for a bear to reach it, even standing on its hind legs.

On another occasion, Carl was camping with only a rucksack and sleeping bag – and a rifle. He was getting his evening meal ready when he noticed a pack of six or eight wolves standing about 30 yards away, just looking at him. He picked up his rifle and loaded it but the wolves made no movement towards him or away. After five minutes. Or so, Carl carried on preparing and then eating his meal. Eventually the wolves moved away but they could be heard not far off. Carl lay down in his sleeping bag and went asleep (something I don't think I would have been able to do in the circumstances).

Next morning, Carl awoke to find that, during the night, the wolves had dragged a leg of a freshly killed deer and left it beside his sleeping bag. I have no idea what wolf thought processes were involved in this incident but I think at that point I would have been heading back to civilisation as fast as I could. Carl, however, simply continued his wilderness holiday for some days more.

Questions And An Appreciation

In shops, petrol stations etc. in the fifties people were served by shop assistants. There was time for conversation while you did your shopping. Nowadays, more and more services and transactions are self-service with little or no human interaction. Banks with their cutbacks in counter staff and introduction of ATMs in branches are a prime example of this. These changes may make for speedier *transactions* but do they actually improve the service to customers? I know that, in these days of computers, it takes five days to clear a cheque paid into your bank account – exactly the same time as in 1962 when my College grant cheque was paid at the start of each term. But in 1962 there were no computers and all transactions were recorded manually, so where is the improvement?

Should we look back and regard the slower pace of life of the fifties and sixties and even later, as hopelessly inefficient or should we regard it as being perhaps more suited to a proper development of human relationships? Have we lost real human contact now that we can be reached "24/7" by e-mail, text or twitter or spend hours in front of a computer screen?

Do girls and boys still spend time in courting, or is everything now, now, now and, if so, is this a good thing? Do children nowadays get too much, too soon? We didn't, simply because the money was not there and so we learned to wait for things.

Will children in an era of "Health and Safety" ever get the chance of wandering round a cash and carry, as I did, and be fascinated by the exotic places food comes from as I was? Will they be allowed at sixteen years old to go off on a field trip and study a river bank as a group of four or five without a teacher being there all the time to supervise and be expected to behave responsibly and actually do so?

Of course, there have been many improvements since I and countless other children were growing up from the 1940s to the 1960s, not least in health, standards of living, ease of travel and communication with people far away. But there was a greater sense of community when I was young in place of the emphasis on individuality that exists today. Then, most people knew most of their neighbours. Today, many people living in cities and towns often do not know the people living more than a few doors away from them. At the age of seventy-one I am glad to have seen poverty, if by no means eradicated, at least greatly reduced. Equally, I am glad to have grown up in what was for many, but not all, children in some ways a golden age of innocence, simplicity, freedom just to be children but with known and generally accepted boundaries of behaviour (at least in principle), increasing access to education and increasing opportunities.

Deo gratias.

Gerald Rice,

August 2014.

P.T.O. ⇨

A Request to Readers

A Time of Our Lives is being self-published by the author and, as you can appreciate, the budget for publicity and marketing is almost non-existent. So, I would like to make a request.

If you have enjoyed this book, as I hope you have, please tell a friend about it. If you use Facebook or Twitter please mention it on these. Consider buying it as a Christmas or birthday present for a parent or relative who can remember at least some of the times depicted, or for anyone who is interested in memories of childhood and more grown up adventure and romance. Of course, it would also be ideal to take away on holiday or just to read at any time of the year.

How To Buy This Book

The book is currently available through the Internet and direct from the author at a price of £9/€10/$15 plus postage in each case. It will also be available as an ebook.

Full information about *A Time of Our Lives* and how to buy it from the Internet can be found at www.atimeofourlives.com

Alternatively you can buy directly from the author, Gerald Rice, at: A Time of Our Lives Limited, 11 Mornington Green, Trim, County Meath, Ireland.

If buying direct, in £ Sterling or Euro, preferred payment method is by Postal Order made payable to Rice. Cheque payments must be cleared before the book can be despatched.

A Time of Our Lives Limited
Tel: 00 353 46 94 366 94 / 046 94 366 94
Mobile: 00 353 86 03 150 84 / 086 03 150 84
E-Mail: info@atimeofourlives.com
            omaolc2009@gmail.com